MW01288901

# PREJUDICE UNVEILED

## THE MYTHS AND REALITIES ABOUT ISLAM

### A. M. AMANA

# PREJUDICE UNVEILED:
## THE MYTHS AND REALITIES ABOUT ISLAM

All rights reserved. No part of this book may be reproduced in any form or by any electronic or mechanical means including information storage and retrieval systems without permission in writing from the copyright holder, except by a reviewer, who may quote brief passages in review.

Includes bibliographical references and index.

Printed in the United States of America by CreateSpace

7290-B Investment Drive

North Charleston, South Carolina 29418

Copyright© 2012 by A. M. Amana

ISBN: 1463701128

ISBN-13: 9781463701123

LCCN: 2010943185

CreateSpace, North Charleston, South Carolina

*To my parents*

It is better to light a candle than to curse the darkness.

*—Chinese proverb*

# CONTENTS

# PROLOGUE

This book is intended for a wide audience, but primarily for non-Muslims who have, for whatever reasons, ingrained misconceptions and misunderstandings about Islam. The book doesn't intend to compete with classical sources about the Muslim faith, and it isn't going to be a detailed account of historical facts and dates. By contrast, the narrative is intertwined with reflections, and is deliberately easy to follow to convey Islam's universal teachings to a Western audience.

The idea about writing this book was brewing in my mind for quite some time. The disastrous events of September 11, 2001, and what has happened after that in the way that many Europeans and Americans view Islam, started to make me feel that Islam and all Muslims are being lumped together into one big heap of misconception. It also became clear that Islam is, and probably always has been, the most misunderstood religion in the world. It's quite sad to see that the perception of

Islam, after more than 1,400 years of existence, still does not accurately reflect the underlying principles and ideologies of this universal faith.

I made the decision to write this book after watching a documentary made in the United States that completely misrepresented the true essence of Islam.[1] I couldn't help but feel deeply disheartened by the incessant prejudice against Muslims fuelled by such distorted media, and knew that I had to do something constructive to try to accurately portray Islam as a tolerant and global religion.

According to the *Oxford American Dictionary* the word "myth" is defined as "A widespread but untrue or erroneous story or belief; a widely held misconception; or a misrepresentation of the truth." The myths about Islam presented in this book are derived from my qualitative research on how non-Muslims incorrectly perceive the Islamic faith. Before writing, I watched biased documentary films that misrepresent Islam, went to numerous anti-Islam web sites, and read many books that portrayed Muslims and their religion in a negative light. In addition, I observed the Western media and how it chooses to report on Muslims. Lastly, I thought about all the queries that my non-Muslim friends, colleagues, and neighbors have been asking about Islam, especially after the horrendous events of September 11. Some of those questions were as follows: "Is it true that Islam is an intolerant religion?" "Wasn't the Quran made up by Muhammad?" "Do Muslims hate Jews and Christians?" and so on. Following this process, I compiled the most common misunderstandings, misconceptions, and allegations about Islam, culminating in nine specific topics, or myths. In my view, these common misunderstandings are myths because they're false notions based on centuries of ignorance about true Islam.

I wrote this book as a Western-educated Muslim and as a neutral observer with a passion for comparative religion and scripture. I believe that if people learn about each other and trust each other, everything else should fall into place. I haven't formally studied religion, and I wouldn't consider myself by any means a conservative Muslim, so it's important for the reader to learn a bit about my background to know which perspective my reasoning is coming from.

My mother, Marianne, was born in northern England and raised as a Protestant. Although not religious, she converted to Islam when she married my father in London in the late 1950s. My father, Muhammad, was born in a small village in the Delta of Egypt. After receiving his PhD in economics in the United States thanks to a scholarship from the Egyptian government, he became a career diplomat. Following retirement, he became a research fellow in international development at a leading university in England, where he has published several books.

As for me, I was born in Italy in the mid-1960s in a Jesuit hospital. My boyhood and adolescence were spent between Egypt and Italy in the 1970s and 1980s. I attended an all-boys Roman Catholic high school, and after graduation I went to Switzerland to get an education in management, then a master's degree in international relations in the United States. I have also lived in England, Portugal, and Dubai, and can speak five languages, including classical Arabic. I reside today in the US with my wife, Jasmine, and two children. In 2005, I went to Mecca to complete the pilgrimage, a profound experience that changed my way of looking at life.

My professional career started out in the nose-to-the-grindstone world of hotel administration, which made little economic sense (to me at least) as a long-term career because of the outrageously long hours and low pay. But since I enjoyed the lodging sector in general, I decided to stay involved on the investment side of the business, advising clients on how to invest their hard-earned cash prudently in property worldwide. Most of my career has been in the US, where I've worked for small private firms and large public corporations, reaching the position of senior vice-president.

Clearly, I don't exactly have a typical background, yet it's been quite transitional and, as a result, I am unbiased when it comes to different cultures, points of view, and faiths. After living in several countries, I've learned two basic principles: ignorance is the root cause of hatred in the world, and people are essentially tribal, with an innate anxiety about those who speak different languages and have different rituals, thinking, and points of reference. I'm convinced that these two fundamental human characteristics are the primary cause for the misunderstandings about Islam. Therefore, this book is an objective attempt to discredit these misinterpretations, bringing to light the true essence of Islam.

# Author's Note

While there is a recognized system for the transliteration of Arabic into English, along with specific diacritical markings to indicate long and short vowels, I have endeavored, for the sake of clarity and ease, to present all Arabic words in their simplest and most recognizable English rendering.

In addition, it is recommended that Muslims mention a specific prayer for the Prophet Muhammad whenever his name is written or mentioned. Therefore, the formula *Salla Allahu alayhi wa sallam* ("may God's peace and blessings be upon him," or sometimes the "pbuh" abbreviation) normally follows the Prophet's name whenever it appears in classical text or biographies. Since this book is addressed to a wide audience, primarily non-Muslims, I shall abstain from inserting it in the text and let any Muslim reader inwardly formulate this prayer as he or she reads.

# MYTH ONE:

## Islam Came to Cancel Other Religions

As living beings, we have no control over when we are born, who our family will be, or when we shall die. The only thing that we know for sure is that after we die our flesh turns to dust. The rest is a mosaic of faith, unproven expectations, and attempts to understand the ungraspable, which inevitably creates anxiety for most of us. As a result of this lack of control, we are constantly dealing with the apprehension that's linked to this everlasting question: what happens to our self-identity when we die? This incessant query is answered in the same way by the three essentially similar divine faiths—their disparity being that they were conveyed to humanity during different periods, and are expressed through different rituals.

Judaism, Christianity, and Islam are sedatives to human-kind. This is because they ease our innate anxiety, answering that perpetual question by telling us that if we do good deeds in our lives, worship God, and follow the teachings of His prophets, our body-soul vessels shall experience serenity and forgiveness after we die, in a completely different dimension of existence. The Quran (pronounced kur-ahn) reduces the angst of Muslims when it says:

*Happy are those who*
*have purified themselves*
*and remember the name*
*of their Lord and pray.*
*But you prefer the life of the world*
*though the hereafter is better*
*and more lasting.*
*That is, indeed, in the earlier books,*
*in the books of Abraham and Moses.*[1]

### THE ESSENCE OF MUHAMMAD'S MESSAGE

The West should calm down and learn to see Islam for what it is, and not keep speculating. In broad outline, Islam believes in the worship of God in five primary ways: accepting fully that He is the one and only God and that the Prophet Muhammad is one of His messengers, prayer, fasting, giving to the needy, and completing the pilgrimage to Mecca once in a lifetime.

Muslims believe that Islam came as an extension and con-tinuation of the essential teachings of Abraham, the prime instigator of monotheism, and the faiths of Judaism and Christianity that preceded it. Islam believes that the three divine religions are essentially one, with a similar message revealed to all of humanity by God via scripture. Islam believes completely in the Jewish conviction and in the original Christian teachings—in the greatness of Moses and Jesus.

> *The Muslims, the Jews, and the Christians,*
> *any who believe in God*
> *and the last day*
> *and do good*
> *have their reward with their Lord.*
> *There is nothing for them to fear.*[2]

The word *Islam* in Arabic means "a state of peaceful surrender," "the submission to the will of God," or "the handing over of something to someone;" the word *Muslim* is the participle of the same verb of which *Islam* is the infinitive. In its context as a divine faith, Islam is a state of being focused on peacefully handing over oneself to a way of life that is in submission to God's teachings and will. It also means to surrender to the notion that we are all created equal to worship God during our brief time in this world, and that we will somehow be judged based on our intentions, actions, and choices, which are the results of our own free will.

According to a recent report by the Pew Forum on Religion & Public Life, there are 1.57 billion Muslims today—making it the second largest religion in the world after Christianity.[3] The Pew Forum report also provides evidence that while the heart of Islam might beat in the Middle East, its greatest numbers lie in Asia. More than 60 percent of the world's Muslims live in Asia, in countries such as Indonesia, Pakistan, and India.

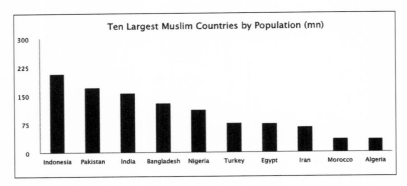

*Source: The Pew Forum on Religion & Public Life*

The Quran is the sacred scripture of Islam and is believed by Muslims to be comprised of the direct words of God that were revealed to Muhammad by the Angel Gabriel over a period of twenty-two years between 610 CE and 632 CE (unless indicated otherwise, all dates in this book are during the Common Era, abbreviated as CE, which is similar to Anno Domini, or AD). The Quran describes many biblical prophets and messengers, such as Adam, Noah, Moses, and Jesus and his apostles. The Quran states that these men had already embraced what Islam was to later reinforce because they submitted to God, preached His message, and upheld His values. Thus, in the Quran, Jesus's disciples tell him, *"We believe in God; witness that we surrender to Him."*[4]

As a moderate Muslim, I believe that life is ultimately a test—a never-ending struggle between the opposing forces of good and bad, the desire to live and the fear of dying, and the urge to hold on to the present and the inevitable letting go.

*And if God wished,*
*God would have made you a single nation;*

*but the intent is to test you*
*in what God has given you.*
*So let your goals*
*be everything good.*[5]

I believe that we exist in this world primarily to love and worship God by contributing constructively to society and by constantly striving for self-improvement: *"And I only created sprites and humans to worship Me."*[6] God, in turn, has set the parameters by which we are to be judged. So that the test is perfect and just, God has deliberately left humans in a position of everlingering doubt about His teachings and even His existence. God has chosen to reveal Himself through scripture, signs, or miracles, but never revealing Himself completely to humanity. It has not occurred throughout history that humans woke up one day and literally saw God appearing in a unified physical form that's comprehensible to the human brain.

But why this ambiguous life and test into which we are brought? Perhaps because God, whose spirit lives within each one of us, relies on the love, worship, and goodness that emanates from His creations in a way that we'll never fully understand. The more God is worshiped and the more that good prevails through all His creations, the more God's existence is eternally sustained. God's spirit is within us and is in constant receptive mode toward us, but it's up to humans to work hard to seek Him out and surrender to His will and teachings—to accept the harsh reality that one day we shall leave this material world and experience the wondrous realm of the unknown.

There is no doubt that Islam is a demanding religion, but when applied with moderation, logic, and common sense, its rewards are immense. Most importantly, Muslims are required to believe in the one and only God (*al-Shahada*) and that Muhammad is one of His messengers to all humankind. In Arabic, the word *Allah* simply means God—the same God of Abraham, Moses, and Jesus.

In addition, Muslims are asked by God to pray to Him five times a day—at dawn, noon, midafternoon, sunset, and at night—with a total of seventeen prayer-cycles. The seventeen prayer-cycles are as follows: two at dawn, four at noon, four in midafternoon, three in the evening, and four at night. Each cycle, which typically lasts for about one minute, basically entails the recitation of verses from the Quran and two yogic prostrations. Foremost, prayer is a means of showing loyalty, gratitude, modesty, and love toward God, reminding Muslims that there is an Almighty who created them and to Whom they can bow their heads in total humility. Another purpose of prayer is to take a "time-out" from the rat race we so easily get caught up in, and to regroup with ourselves and with the Creator. It has been medically proven that prayer is beneficial to the heart and spine, and increases the capacity for memory and attention.[7]

When I was working in Dubai, there was a small prayer room on the upper floor of the office building, which is quite common in the Middle East. Each time after performing prayer, I would feel much more relaxed and focused, ready to return to work with a keener outlook. Prayer also serves as a way to unite families and communities, and that's why group prayers are encouraged over solo ones. Similar to fasting, prayer is not forced upon Muslims who are sick, under duress, or traveling. For example, the seventeen daily prayer-cycles are reduced to eleven for those who are traveling more than fifty miles from home, and women who are menstruating are completely exempt from prayer.

Muslims are also required to fast from dawn to dusk during the holy month of Ramadan (the month in which the first verses of the Quran were revealed to Muhammad) to learn patience and discipline; to know how the poor and hungry feel without food or clean water; and to abstain from instant gratifications such as sex, smoking, or lustfully eyeing a woman or a man. Fasting for religious and spiritual reasons has been part of human custom since prehistory. It's mentioned in the Old Testament and New Testament, as well as the Hindu Mahabharata. Fasting is practiced in many other religious traditions and spiritual practices, and is medically proven to enhance the body's metabolism.[8] This is because the stomach and intestines are given a nearly twelve-hour break and are cleansed, which can have a positive impact on people's overall sense of well-being.

Fasting is by no means easy. Actually, I have found fasting to be the most difficult commandment in Islam, perhaps because I started to fast when I was twenty-three, compared to the majority of Muslims who start at the early age of ten or twelve, making their bodies accustomed to it earlier.

I'll never forget the first day I fasted. It was in the hot and humid summer of 1988 in Madison, Wisconsin, where I was visiting an Italian friend attending college there. My friend, Giovanni, was a talented cook and he wanted to make sure I ate well at the end of my first day of fasting, so he labored in the kitchen from around three in the afternoon until sunset, creating a variety of pastas, salads, and delicious meat dishes. By noon that day, I was totally comatose because I didn't have the recommended predawn light meal for sustenance and was aching for caffeine. I slept most of the day, and then one hour before sunset I gave in and decided I couldn't take it anymore. So I rushed downstairs to a small Greek tavern, and after gobbling down a huge gyro and drinking several sodas, I felt so bloated that I had to find a place to lie flat on my back. I wandered off to a park by the scenic University of Wisconsin campus to recuperate, feeling guilty about breaking the fast early and about Giovanni's missed dinner. I eventually went back to his apartment and apologized extensively for not showing up. Surprisingly, he was quite understanding and encouraging. He told me how next time I would be able to overcome my lack of patience and have more discipline over my cravings, which eventually became true.

When I end the fast now during Ramadan, I experience a sense of satisfaction, spiritual uplifting, and accomplishment for not giving in to my hunger, thirst, and caffeine addiction— a kind of victory of mind over matter. When I end the fast, I have a glass of warm milk and some dates, perform the sunset prayer, and then slowly start eating a full meal, trying to humbly emulate the way the Prophet would break his fast. (I must confess, however, that some days during Ramadan I still fall off the wagon and break the fast early).

It is important to know that fasting is not ruthlessly imposed upon those Muslims who are sick, traveling, or under any kind of physical or emotional duress, such as pregnant women or the mentally ill. If unable to fast, a Muslim is allowed to give as charity an amount that is equal to providing a basic meal at the prevailing cost in that person's country. In the United States, for example, this amount is widely accepted as approximately fifteen dollars. So if a Muslim is unable to fast for, say, ten days during Ramadan, he or she would need to make this up by giving $150 to the needy, and so on.

In addition to surrendering themselves to the one and only God, prayer, and fasting Muslims are required to give 2.5 percent of their annual savings as an almsgiving (*zaka*) to the needy. Paying zaka has two important benefits: it helps the poor and it purifies a Muslim's income. If money isn't available to donate as charity, Muslims can give food or material possessions instead. In Islam, it's wrong to build a private fortune selfishly at the expense of others, and good to share wealth fairly. Muslims are also encouraged to create a just society where poor people are treated with respect.

The pilgrimage to Mecca (*hajj*) is by no means some kind of medieval ritual that Muslims tick off from their to-do list. The hajj is a five-day, physically intensive, spiritually demanding obligation that should be carried out at least once in a lifetime by every able-bodied Muslim who can afford to do so. It is also a demonstration of the solidarity of the Muslim people and their submission to God. Although the hajj is associated with the life of Muhammad in the seventh century, the ritual of pilgrimage to Mecca is considered by Muslims to stretch back circa four thousand years to the time of Abraham, who is believed to have built the *Kaaba* (the black, shrouded, cuboidal structure) with his son Ishmael. The Kaaba was an important site even before the rise of Islam, and it was revered as a sacred symbol and sanctuary that celebrated both monotheism and idolatry over different eras. Today, the Kaaba is a symbol of monotheism and the central place that God has in the life of all Muslims. The sight of thousands of people circling the Kaaba during the hajj (always seven times and counterclockwise) is as if one is watching a beautiful body of water swirling round its vortex. With the low humming sound emanating from the thousands of worshippers, the impressiveness of this sight is further enhanced by the occasional view of a flock of small birds flying in unison above the circulating pilgrims.

During the hajj, pilgrims must be in a state of *ihraam* (consecration). Men wear two pieces of white unstitched cloth which are similar to a shroud, one covering the waist and legs, and the other around the shoulders covering the upper body. Women can wear any type of clothing, as long as it covers all their bodies except their faces and hands, and it's not tight or transparent. While in ihraam, pilgrims must not cut their hair or nails, wear perfumes, kill animals or insects, or engage in any kind of sexual relations (including proposals of marriage). Pilgrims are also not allowed to get angry, have any arguments, or curse. Hence, an overall sense of unity and serenity, known as *sakina* in Arabic, is experienced during the pilgrimage.

In many ways, the hajj is not dissimilar to a global convention that brings together millions of people from all nationalities in a peaceful and orderly manner, where the attendees submit themselves to God as equals and as imperfect mortals, asking for His forgiveness. When I was in Mecca in 2005, I met an old man who barely spoke any English, but was able to joyously convey that he'd come all the way from Serbia in a small van, and that he'd been saving all his life to come to Mecca. There were probably thousands there like him from all over the world, highlighting that Islam is a global faith that believes in the peaceful unity of humanity—a faith with common aspirations, anxieties, and fears that are similar to those of the Jews, Hindus, Buddhists, and Christians. A study published in 2009 by researchers at Harvard University's Kennedy School of Government found that the hajj leads to a sense of greater harmony among ethnic groups and Islamic sects, and to more favorable attitudes toward women, including greater acceptance of female education and employment.

The most moving ritual of the hajj for me was at Mount Arafat. Mount Arafat is where Muslims stand on the second day of the pilgrimage in contemplative vigil, near a hill outside Mecca from which Muhammad gave his Farewell Sermon. This is when pilgrims are required to spend their time praying and thinking about the course of their lives and the inevitable arrival of a day when they shall depart this world. The fact that all male pilgrims are dressed in identical white shrouds—to accentuate Islam's credo that we're all born as equals and to remind people of when they'll eventually be buried in similar shrouds—adds to the moment's spiritual profoundness. Standing there at the foot of Mount Arafat, surrounded by millions of pilgrims in silent prayer and solemn contemplation, I started to cry. My mind unraveled with moments from my childhood, memories of loved ones who've passed away, and thoughts of my two children and the mistakes I've made. It was the first time in my life that I completely came to terms with my mortality, fully accepting myself with all my faults and attributes. The Mount Arafat experience is a soul-baring one-on-one with God, which is intended to leave Muslims spiritually reborn.

The symbolic stoning of the devil is also a significant ritual of the hajj. At a place near Mecca called Mina the pilgrims perform *ramye al-jamarat*, throwing small stones to signify their defiance of the devil and humanity's constant struggle between good and bad. This symbolizes the trials experienced by Abraham while he decided whether to sacrifice his son Ishmael as demanded by God. The devil challenged him three times, and three times Abraham refused. Later in time, three pillars were erected to mark the location of each one of those refusals. Because of the massive crowds (an estimated three million pilgrims perform the hajj annually), the pillars were replaced in 2004 by long walls with catch basins to collect the stones that are being thrown at the universal symbol of evil.

Contrary to Western perception, the requirements of the Muslim faith are not oppressive obligations. Rather, they are pragmatic rituals, wherein the believer is responsible only for those tasks that he or she is able to perform, as elucidated in 2:286 of the Quran: *"Our Lord, do not charge us with a burden like that You laid upon those before us, and do not impose on us what we cannot bear."* The most important factor in the performance of any Muslim ritual is the worshipper's sincere intention toward God.

In addition to the five duties incumbent on every Muslim (known as the Five Pillars of Islam, which were established more than two hundred years after the death of the Prophet), followers of the Muslim faith are required to attend communal prayer and a sermon on Fridays at a mosque; they must guard their ears from slander and obscenity, their tongues from lies; they are required to refrain from cursing or sneering at others; they mustn't harm other creations; and their hearts should remain free of envy, anger, and hypocrisy.

## THE MYSTIQUE OF MEDINA

Although not part of the hajj ritual itself, most Muslims visit Medina before or after the pilgrimage to pay homage to the Prophet Muhammad. Medina, 210 miles north of Mecca, is where Muhammad is buried and where the original Mosque of the Prophet is located. Medina is probably one of the most spiritually serene places on earth, exuding a sense of calmness that overcomes pilgrims because they actually get to see the Prophet's home, as well as his tomb which is adjacent to those of two of his closest companions, Abou Bakr al-Sudeeq (d. 634) and Omar ibn al-Khattab (d. 644).

Medina is surreal in many ways, as one can almost feel the presence of the Prophet. A sense of tranquility and serenity that I had never experienced before enveloped me there, making me feel that I finally understood and knew Muhammad as a person. I could feel his aura within my essence, and aspired to capture it, to take it with me for the rest of my life.

The magnificent Mosque of the Prophet is the second holiest in Islam and the second largest in the world after the Masjid al-Haram in Mecca. The mosque in Medina was originally built by the Prophet in 622, and subsequent Islamic rulers vastly expanded and decorated it. The edifice was originally Muhammad's modest house where he settled after his emigration (*hijra*) to Medina, later building a mosque on its grounds. He himself shared in the heavy work of its construction.

As it stands today, the Mosque of the Prophet has a rectangular plan on two floors with the prayer hall projecting toward the south and occupying the entire first floor. The mosque's enclosure is about one hundred times bigger than the original house of prayer built by the Prophet and can accommodate more than five hundred thousand worshippers at any given time.

The Mosque of the Prophet is topped with twenty-four white domes with holes pierced into the base of each dome that illuminate the serene interior. The roof is also used for prayer during peak times, and when the twenty-four domes slide out on metal tracks to shade areas of the roof, they create beautiful light wells for the vast prayer hall.

The mosque is elegantly decorated with polychrome marble and stones. The columns are of white marble with brass capitals supporting slightly pointed arches, built of black and white stones. As mentioned, the Mosque of the Prophet contains the original house of prayer built by Muhammad. The two sections can be easily distinguished: the older section has many colorful decorations and numerous small pillars; the new section is in gleaming white marble.

The most notable feature of the mosque is the green Dome of the Prophet, which is higher than the twenty-four white domes. This is where the tomb of Muhammad is located. At the heart of the mosque is a small area called *al-Rawda al-Nabawiya*, which extends from the tomb of the Prophet to his original wooden pulpit. Entrance into al-Rawda is not always possible (especially during the hajj), as the tiny area can accommodate only a few hundred people. The green fence at the tomb of Muhammad is guarded by Saudi volunteers who prevent pilgrims from touching the fence, which is regarded as idolatry in Islam.

### THE CURRENT PROBLEMS OF MUSLIMS

When Christianity, Judaism, and Islam were initially conveyed to humanity, they were pure and perfect. With the passing of time, we flawed humans have diverted from the original messages of these great religions. Alas, over the centuries, extremist waves of thought, application, and interpretation in all three divine faiths have assumed to have a monopoly on what is right and what is wrong.

Muhammad al-Ghazzali (d. 1996), the Egyptian theologian, said in an interview on state television in the 1950s that "Islam is a just case in the hands of failed attorneys." What al-Ghazzali believed is ever-so-relevant today. This is because the current prejudice against Islam is not only a result of the West's lack of understanding toward this religion, but is due to the fact that radical, militant puritans have strayed from the true essence of Islam in such a way that it fans the fires of hatred from the West, resulting in the widespread myths about its teachings. An extreme and perverse ideology in the minds of its fanatics is what directly threatens Islam today, namely the radicals in such countries as Saudi Arabia, Afghanistan, and Pakistan, among others. Accompanying this threat of religious extremism is a global crisis of misunderstanding toward the Muslim faith.

Due to a complex web of sociopolitical problems, namely rampant corruption and a belief that Western culture has failed them, radical and militant Islamic groups have turned into fascists. These radical groups, like the Nazis in Germany, are trying to woo uneducated young women and men by combining religious zeal with mob violence. The fanaticism that we see in modern Islam is a new development in a religion that, in its early history, was famous for its tolerance and respect for other faiths. In Islam's classical period in medieval Spain and Egypt, perhaps only Buddhism rivaled Islam's tolerance.

The extremism that characterizes the behavior of radical Muslims today is in fact anti-Quranic. Whenever the Muslim militants commit atrocities in the name of made-up Islam, some Muslim countries refuse to condemn them (at least officially). Islamic countries must ask their governments and the influential Organization of the Islamic Conference (OIC) to openly condemn these radicals, declaring them as the enemies of Islam. This will have the powerful effect of these militant groups having to explain their ludicrous views on violence, women, and social justice. Moreover, the *sharia*, the body of Islamic laws which was never intended to violate human rights and is there for the good of mankind, is manipulated by these extremist groups for their selfish, destructive motives. As such, it is completely unjust to say that Islam *per se* is the problem; rather, it is the skewed interpretation and application of Islam by extremist Muslims, coupled with the West's misinterpretation of Islam, that are the biggest problems. That is, the myths about Islam that have calcified over the centuries in Europe and the US have been indirectly fuelled by Muslims who fail to grasp the true essence of Islam, which teaches one to be lenient toward others and to understand their value systems. The essence of tolerance, preached by Muhammad in the seventh century and available for everyone to interpret in their own way in the Quran, is embedded in these words: *"For you, your religion; for me, my religion."* [9]

Religious fanatics—either purposely or out of ignorance—have perverted their interpretation of Islam into a creed of intolerance and hatred toward the West. They justify their brutality with bizarre interpretations of the Quran, the Prophet's sayings (*hadith*), and the eyewitness "reports" of the maxims and customary practice (*sunna*) of Muhammad to serve their political, financial, and power-hungry agendas. They distort the true teachings of the Prophet by insisting that all Muslims must not separate Islam from politics, subduing anyone who doesn't share their extremist views regardless of nationality or religion.

Unfortunately, vulnerable Muslims incorrectly sympathize with their violent actions, or join in the connivance of silence. This crisis of misunderstanding of Islam—by some Muslims themselves—has been compounded by the failure of corrupt governments, skeptical people of other faiths, and the vast majority of well-intentioned Muslims which resists, isolates, and discredits these dangerous ideologies. The crisis, therefore, afflicts Muslims and non-Muslims alike with dire consequences, and the failure to understand the true nature of Islam will permit the continued radicalization of Muslims on a global scale. As a result, most Muslims today are in a down-cycle. That is, their application of Islam is in bad shape, and it's up to Muslims to confront the current wave of decline and misinterpretation of their own religion and look to the future for change and reform. Muslims (including myself) need to look closely in the mirror and confront their weaknesses and address the threats that they face globally, in tandem with their strengths and opportunities.

## SWOT ANALYSIS

In graduate school, I learned a basic tool called SWOT Analysis.[10] SWOT Analysis is typically used as a strategic planning tool to evaluate the strengths, weaknesses, opportunities, and threats involved in a project or business venture. I have found the SWOT Analysis method to be useful in assessing not only business projects, but essentially any topic, situation, or even creed, such as Islam. The following table provides a SWOT Analysis of the current state of Islam, highlighting the weaknesses inherent in the way that Muslims are dealing with their religion in today's world, as well as the numerous threats they face. The weaknesses that are highlighted are based on my own experiences and interactions with Muslims in different countries over time. They are not in any way intended to be negative or stereotypical observations—to the contrary, they are an objective assessment of the underlying sociopolitical and cultural trends that provide an opening for Muslims to improve. And to improve, Muslims today have to be self-critical, humble, and willing to accept that all humans are imperfect.

One of the many opportunities that Muslims can seize is to accurately convey to the West that Islam is a divine faith with many common values with Judaism and Christianity, two religions that were also introduced gradually to humanity.

## Islam Came to Confirm God's Message

God selected to communicate with humankind via scripture in gradual phases throughout different eras—through Abraham, Moses, Jesus, and lastly, Muhammad. There were, of course, many prophets who came in between, but these four messengers were the foremost conduits between God and humanity. There was a timely reason for the introduction of God's religions, and the phased renewal of His divine messages was essential to adapt to the different conditions and circumstances that were unfolding during their respective times.

The logic behind this process was probably to gradually introduce the extremely demanding teachings of virtue, and the strict ways of dealing with the messy and harsh realities of the human condition. Simply, God was being kind to humanity by applying this measured approach, because He knows that it takes generations to change ways of ingrained thinking.

| SWOT ANALYSIS—ISLAM AND MUSLIMS TODAY | |
|---|---|
| **STRENGTHS OF ISLAM** | **WEAKNESSES OF MUSLIMS** |
| Only one version of the Quran. | High rates of ignorance, poverty, and illiteracy. |
| The Quran, which is believed to be the word of God, is capable of multiple interpretations throughout different eras. | Lack of unity. |
| | Occasional reliance on weak hadith. |
| Founded by the Prophet Muhammad, the most influential person in history and the only leader who was supremely successful on both the religious and secular levels.[11] | Self-victimization and an obsession with the past glory of the Islamic Caliphate (634–1258). |
| | Inability to separate religion from politics. |
| No hierarchical religious clergy that necessitates an intermediation between God and Muslims. | The rift between Shia and Sunni Muslims. |
| Preaches universal values: faith in God, peace, fraternity among people, pluralism, human rights, democracy, racial equality, love for parents, and ethics at the service of all beings, among many others. | Literal interpretation of outmoded ideologies and attitudes that need urgent reform and renewal. |
| | Dominated by backward-thinking, older, male scholars who promote a diminished role for women in society. |
| Its inherent capacity to come to terms with other religions and tolerate them. | Tendency to live in isolated societies in the West that are not well integrated into Western culture. |
| Vast and rich history of contributions to Western civilization. | Highly superstitious, with a strong belief in conspiracies, the "evil eye," and "jinx." |
| Communal religion that is dedicated to the strengthening and preservation of the family. | Reluctance to accept criticism on religious matters. |
| Second largest and fastest-growing religion in the world. | Excessive reliance on superficial media and rumors for information. |
| Open discussion of human mortality. | At times overly fatalistic. |

| OPPORTUNITIES FOR MUSLIMS | THREATS TO MUSLIMS |
| --- | --- |
| Openly renounce violence and take a more unified stance against Muslim extremists. | Radical Muslims, in their desperate struggle to survive, make religion a tool of oppression and violence. |
| Increased cultural assimilation with the West. | The denial of democracy in the majority of Muslim countries has led to the emergence of Islamic extremism and dangerous political Islam. |
| Separate religion and politics. | |
| New dialogue with Jews and Christians. | The abuse of sharia laws by militant extremists who want to establish a utopian, cross-border Muslim community based on political Islam. |
| Ongoing theological reforms and breaking away from the past. | |
| Accurately convey to the West that Islam is a divine faith with many common values with Judaism and Christianity. | A majority of Muslims is convinced that the West (which has been interested only in a stability based on regional dictators, the security of Israel, and affordable oil) is engaged in a war against Islam. |
| Muslim countries can be modern and Islamic (e.g., Turkey and Indonesia). | The revolutions in Tunisia, Egypt, and Libya may not be a smooth pathway to democratic and representative government. |
| Launch a major public relations campaign to improve the image of Islam globally. | |
| Capitalize on the Obama administration's reaching out to the Muslim world. | Prolongation of the bad press and incessant stereotyping that Muslims receive from the Western media. |
| Use the vast amounts of wealth accumulated through oil to build museums and religious centers in the West to showcase Islam's extensive contributions to Western civilization. | Ongoing fear and oppression of Islam will distort the image of Muslims even more. |
| | Continued deterioration of educational institutions. |
| Apply real democracy and pluralism, and adopt successful Western doctrines (such as the United States Constitution). | Excessive materialism, initially imposed by the West. |
| | Rampant corruption at all levels of society. |

Hence, the phased gap of some 600 years between Abraham and Moses; nearly 1,500 years between Moses and Jesus; and approximately 600 years between Jesus and Muhammad, as well as the prophets who came in between, such as Noah, Aaron, Joseph, Jonah, and David, among many others.

The Quran insists strongly that *"there is no compulsion in religion"*[12] and commands Muslims to respect the beliefs of Jews and Christians, whom the Quran calls the "People of the Book," or people of a previous revelation. Thus, it is important to appreciate that Islam did not come to cancel other religions, as is commonly thought in the West—or as is quite often claimed by extremist Muslim groups. This myth has stubbornly survived over the centuries, creating misunderstandings in an already-skeptical Western audience that is bombarded by its media's relentless anti-Islamic messages.

As highlighted earlier, this myth has, ironically, been fuelled by radical Muslims who incorrectly interpret the Quran and the coexistential essence of Islam. When it comes to the false notion that Islam came to erase other religions, these extremists assume that since Islam was the final divinely revealed religion, all the previous creeds are therefore inferior. That is totally absurd. Islam came to confirm and enhance both Judaism and Christianity, and it is purely the last communication in a series of phased contacts between God and humankind.

Because Islam was the last in the trilogy of the divine faiths, it has been subjected to more intense criticism and false accusations than the previous religions, even though Islam came *"…to you with truth verifying the scripture that came before it, and preserving it."*[13] The Quran addresses all people and calls upon humankind to believe in the religion of God, which is aggregated in the messages of Judaism, Christianity, and Islam. This appeal is as clear as daylight in the Quran:

*"We have sent you [Muhammad]*
*only as a mercy to all humanity."*[14]

Moreover, the Quran falsifies the myth that Muhammad's message came to cancel other faiths in several other verses, namely:

*People of scripture, Our messenger has come to you*
*clarifying for you*
*after an intermission in the messengers,*
*lest you say "No bearer of good news*
*has come to us, and no warner."*
*So a bearer of good news*
*and a warner has come to you.*[15]

The Quran reminds Muslims that Muhammad did not come to contradict previous prophets, or to start a totally new faith: *"So remind; you [Muhammad] are but one who reminds."*[16] The Prophet's message of benevolence, compassion, and social justice is the same as that of Abraham, Moses, and Jesus. The Quran mentions only those prophets who were familiar to the Arabs at the time, but today Islamic scholars believe that had Muhammad known about the Buddhists, the Hindus, or even the Native Americans, the Quran would have endorsed their wise ones, too. This is because all rightly guided religions that advocate justice and equality emanated from the same divine source. Consequently, Muhammad never asked Jews or Christians to convert to Islam unless they wished to do so, because he knew that they had received completely valid revelations of their own.

The Prophet himself never said that Islam came to cancel other religions. In fact, he was fully aware that he was merely a mortal messenger sent by God as a clarifier, warner, and a reminder. The first time that Muhammad openly conveyed his message to the people of Mecca in 612, he revealed, "*I am the messenger of God to all humanity.*"[17] The universality of Islam is supported by the fact that Moses is mentioned 136 times in the Quran, Abraham 69 times, Mary 34 times, and Jesus 25 times, while Muhammad is mentioned only four times by name. This also supports that Islam's divine message was sent to *all* people from the beginning of his prophethood, and that Muhammad never claimed that Islam was intended to be a religion for Arabs only. Today, Arabic-speaking people comprise only 20 percent of the world's total Muslim population, and the country with the largest population of Muslims is Indonesia, with some 203 million followers.[18]

### CONCLUSION

The relationship between a human being and God is a personal and intimate bond:

> *We did indeed create the human being,*
> *and We know what his ego suggests;*
> *and We are closer to him*
> *than his jugular vein.*[19]

For that reason, it is arrogant and self-righteous to assume that one religion has a monopoly on the "absolute truth," and it is a fundamental flaw for any group—whether Orthodox Jews, Evangelical Christians, or Wahhabi Muslims—to create a religious meritocracy with a myopic "us-versus-them" attitude.

The Quran teaches us that all humans are born equal, and whether someone is a Jew, Hindu, Buddhist, Christian, or Muslim should not matter, as it is only through our intentions and deeds that we shall be judged by God. And that is the true essence of Islam.

# MYTH TWO:

### The Quran is Not a Miracle

During his travels to Syria as a successful young merchant, Muhammad ibn Abdullah (c. 570–632) had been introduced to the teachings of Judaism, Christianity, and the Hanifs, those who believed in the monotheistic teachings of Abraham. In his late thirties, Muhammad took to regularly visiting a small cave called Hiraa in Mount Nour, or the Mountain of Light, on the outskirts of Mecca. In this cave, the Prophet sought solitude and contemplation on the worrying state of the world he lived in, and the meaning of the messages of Abraham, Moses, and Jesus. On a more local level, he was deeply concerned with the belligerent tribes of Mecca and their total moral bankruptcy.

### REVELATION

On the night of the twenty-seventh of the Arabian month of Ramadan in 610 (known as the Night of Power), and at the age of forty, Muslims believe that the first communication between Muhammad and God commenced, via the Angel Gabriel. On his first encounter, Gabriel, who appeared in supernatural form with a sheet of cloth with written verses on it, said to Muhammad, "*Iqraa*," meaning "Read!" The Prophet replied, "I cannot read," as he had not received any formal education and did not know how to read or write. The Angel Gabriel then embraced Muhammad so tightly that he nearly lost his consciousness. After releasing the Prophet, Gabriel said, "Read!" once again. The Prophet's answer was the same as before, "I cannot read," and Gabriel repeated the embrace for the last time. Gabriel then showed Muhammad the words that were on the sheet of cloth, which were to be the first revealed verses of the Holy Quran:

> *Read, in the name of your Lord, who created:*
> *created man of clotted blood.*
> *Read, for your Lord is most generous,*
> *the one who taught the use of the pen,*
> *taught man what he did not know.*[1]

Muhammad was so terrified by the whole experience of the revelation and the sight of Gabriel that he had to flee the cave of Mount Nour. His mind was racing and he began to wonder if he was possessed. Afraid that his family would think he was indeed demon-possessed, he considered throwing himself down a mountain to end his life, but he heard a voice saying that he was an apostle of God. When he reached his home, emotionally drained and shivering from fear and cold sweat, he told his wife Khadija, "Cover me, cover me!" After his awe had somewhat abated, Khadija asked him about the reason for his heightened anxiety and fear. After he told her his terrifying experience, she assured him by saying, "God will not let you down, because you are kind to relatives, you speak only the truth, you help the poor, the orphans, and the needy, and you are an honest man." She then took him to Waraqa ibn Nawfal, her cousin, who was a Christian and an old, saintly man with knowledge of previous revelations and scripture. Waraqa asked the Prophet, "What did you see?" When Muhammad told him, Waraqa replied, "That is the same angel whom God sent to the Prophet Moses. Should I live until you receive the divine message, I will support you strongly." After a few days, Waraqa died.[2] For the first two years after the initial revelation, Muhammad kept quiet about his experience. He had new revelations, but confided only in his wife Khadija. It was only in 612 that Muhammad felt empowered to preach, and gradually started to gain converts.

The Quranic experiences were painful to Muhammad, who, according to the religious scholar Jalal al-Din al-Suyuti (d. 1505), said, "Never once did I receive a revelation without thinking that my soul had been torn away from me." In the early days, the impact was so frightening that his whole body would convulse. He would often sweat copiously, even on a cold day, experience a great heaviness, or hear mysterious sounds of clanking metal and bells in the background.[3] Occasionally, when absorbing the revelations, the state of the Prophet was so distressing that he would cover himself so his companions would not witness him in a tumultuous state.

Other times Gabriel would reveal verses to Muhammad when he was alone, in the form of a beautiful man dressed in a robe, or would come to the Prophet in his dreams. To try and accurately explain what Muhammad was physically, mentally, and spiritually going through is impossible. But perhaps it could be described as the equivalent of being in such a mystical state of mind that it enabled the Prophet to delve deeply and painfully into the inner spheres of his consciousness to be able to receive communication from another dimension of existence. In other words, he was perfectly positioned spiritually at the intersection of the material world and the intangible world.

## STRUCTURE

In Arabic, the Quran means "the reading" or "recitation." The Quran is comprised of 6,236 verses of varying length and 77,701 words, contained within 114 chapters (*suras*). It was revealed gradually by God through the Angel Gabriel to Muhammad in Arabic only over a period of twenty-two years (610 to 632), or an average of five verses a week. Approximately 75 percent of the Quran's 114 chapters were communicated to the Prophet when he was living in Mecca, with the balance revealed after he emigrated to Medina. Each verse was revealed for a specific purpose, situation, or event during those twenty-two years. Some verses should be interpreted only in their own seventh-century context; that is, they are only applicable to the time of Muhammad. In turn, most other verses are to be used as a universal moral benchmark for all eras.

The task that Muhammad was given by God to attract people to Islam was both arduous and enormous. But his mission eventually succeeded, and the Quran itself was an excellent way to convince non-Muslims of his message, aided by his charismatic personality and innate honesty. Muhammad had to broadcast Islam and its message via the Quran, and with the assistance of God, he had to ensure that his message was relevant to his era, as well as universal and timeless enough to be successfully conveyed to future generations until the end of time.

## COMPILATION

One of the common misunderstandings about the Quran is that Othman ibn Affan (d. 656), the third *caliph* (leader) of Islam, authenticated and compiled one Quran from a large set of mutually contradicting copies, and that it was authenticated and written under his personal supervision. I shall examine the roots of this misconception, which says that Othman had the Quran authenticated based on his own whim and interpretation.

Whenever the Prophet received a revelation, he would first memorize it himself and then declare the revelation; he would then instruct his companions to also memorize it. The Prophet would immediately ask scribes to write down the revelation he had received, and he would reconfirm it himself. Muhammad could not read or write, remaining illiterate throughout his life. Therefore, after memorizing each revelation, he would repeat it to his companions. They would write down the verse and he would check it by asking them to read what they had written. If there was any mistake, the Prophet would immediately point it out and have it corrected. Similarly, he would even recheck and authenticate the portions of the Quran memorized by his companions. In this way, the complete Quran was initially written down under the personal supervision of the Prophet Muhammad, not Othman.

The Quran was revealed portion by portion, as and when it was required. It's important to know that the Quran was not compiled by the Prophet in the chronological order of revelation. Rather, the order and sequence of the Quran was divinely inspired and was transmitted to the Prophet by God through the Angel Gabriel. As such, whenever a revelation was conveyed to his companions, the Prophet would also mention in which chapter and after which verse the new revelation should fit.

Every Ramadan, all the portions of the Quran that had been revealed, including the order of the verses, were revised and reconfirmed by the Prophet with the Angel Gabriel. During the last Ramadan before the death of Muhammad in 632, the Quran was reconfirmed twice in its aggregate between Gabriel and the Prophet. It is, therefore, evident that the Quran was compiled and authenticated by Muhammad himself during his lifetime, both in the written form as well as in the memory of many of his companions. At the time of his death, there were twenty-two Muslims who memorized the Quran in its entirety, known as *huffaz*.

The complete Quran, along with the correct sequence of the verses, was in existence during the life of the Prophet. The verses, however, were written on separate pieces—scraps of leather; thin, flat stones; leaflets; palm branches; and animal shoulder blades. After the death of the Prophet, Abou Bakr al-Sudeeq, the first caliph of Islam, ordered that the Quran be copied from all the different materials onto a common material and placed in the shape of sheets. These were tied with strings so that nothing of the compilation was lost.

Many companions of the Prophet would write down the revelation of the Quran on their own whenever they heard it directly from the Prophet. All the verses revealed to Muhammad may not have been heard personally by all the companions simultaneously. There were high possibilities of different portions of the Quran being missed by those companions who were not present during the revelations. This eventually gave rise to disputes among Muslims regarding the different contents of the Quran during the subsequent period of the caliph Othman, nineteen years after the death of the Prophet.

Accordingly, in 651 Othman borrowed the original manuscript of the Quran—which was authorized and canonized by the Prophet—from Hafsa, one of Muhammad's wives. Othman set up a sophisticated Quranic committee to publish a definitive compiled copy of the holy book. He ordered several companions, who were among the scribes who wrote the Quran when the Prophet dictated its verses, to verify and compile the holy book of Islam, a lengthy process led by Zaid ibn Thabit and Ubay ibn Kaab who supervised the rewriting of the script in several perfect copies. Upon completion, these copies were sent by Othman to the emerging centers of Islam at the time, namely Baghdad.

There were other personal collections of the portions of the Quran that people had with them. These might have been incomplete and with mistakes. Therefore, Othman appealed to the people to destroy all these copies, which did not match the original manuscript of the Quran, in order to preserve its original text. Only two copies of the text of the original Quran authenticated by the Prophet himself are present to this day—one at a museum in Tashkent (in the ex-Soviet Union) and the other at the Topkapi Museum in Istanbul, Turkey.

The original manuscript of the Quran does not have the signs indicating the vowels in Arabic script. These vowels are known as *tashkil*. The Arabs did not require the vowel signs and diacritical marks for correct pronunciation of the Quran since it was their mother tongue. For Muslims of non-Arab origin, however, it was difficult to recite the Quran correctly without the necessary vowels. These marks were introduced into the original Quranic script during the time of the fifth caliph, Abd el-Malik ibn Marawan (d. 705).

## THE ABROGATED VERSES

Some skeptics argue that the copy of the Quran that we have today is not the same Quran that was present at the Prophet's time. But they should realize that the word "Quran" in Arabic means a "recitation." Therefore, the preservation of the recitation of the Quran is important, irrespective of whether the script contains vowels or not. If the pronunciation and the Arabic are the same, the meaning remains the same, too. Moreover, God has promised, "*We have, without doubt, sent down the Message; and We will assuredly guard it [from corruption].*"[4] As such, Muslims believe that there is only one version of the Quran and no word in it has been changed over the centuries. This brings us to the so-called abrogated verses of the Quran that have caused much misunderstanding in the West pertaining to its divinity.

The word "abrogation" in Arabic is *naskh*. The word naskh has two meanings: 1) transformation and shifting from one place to another, and 2) cancellation and repeal. In technical terms, abrogation means to cancel and annul some fixed moral rulings and to replace them with new rulings and orders. God says, *"We do not cancel any revelation, or cause it to be forgotten, unless We bring one better, or its equivalent."*[5] He also conveys,

> *When We replace a revelation by another*
> *—and God knows best the divine revelation—*
> *they [the disbelievers] say,*
> *"You [Muhammad] are a mere forger."*
> *But most of them don't know the truth.*
> *Say the holy spirit [Gabriel]*
> *has revealed the truth from your Lord*
> *as guidance and good news.*[6]

Abrogation in the Quran can be in any of the following modes: 1) to cancel a ruling and keep the initial text for reading or reference only, 2) to cancel a ruling and the text as well, or 3) to cancel only the text but not the ruling. In other words, abrogation is primarily related to orders and prohibitions, not the underlying tidings. As for the actual number of abrogations, Jalal al-Din al-Suyuti, in his book *Al-Itqaan* (or *Achieving Proficiency*), mentions that thirty verses were abrogated, or only 0.5 percent of the total number of verses in the Quran.[7] An example of such abrogated verses is shown in the following table.

| INITIAL VERSE | ABROGATED VERSE |
|---|---|
| *"Believers, do not approach prayer while you are intoxicated, until you know what you are saying."* (4:43) | *"Believers—Wine, gambling and idolatry and divination are nothing but abomination from the work of Satan, so avoid them that you may thrive. Satan only wants to sow hostility and hatred among you with wine and gambling, and to hinder you from remembrance of God, and from prayer. So will you refrain?"* (5:90–91) |

As for the wisdom behind abrogation, scholars of Islam have indicated that change is the nature of existence and beings, and abrogation is one of the divine ways to address these changes. If abrogation is reasonable to apply to human beings, as they are subject to change, then it should not be considered strange concerning the rulings about them since Islam's interpretation of the Quran should be constantly evolving and advancing toward what is better and applicable to current times.

Thus, abrogation constitutes a step toward what is better and superior. Abrogation is often a means of bringing ease, since Muslims were required to follow what is higher, stronger, and better in the first stages of their Islamic education and the building of their communities. The abrogation of rulings constituted a form of relief, of soothing, and cancellation of hardship: *"If We wished, We would take away what We have revealed to you by inspiration."* [8]

The Quran was revealed gradually for specific events and under different circumstances, and as events during the lifetime of Muhammad unfolded, enhanced verses were revealed in tandem with the gradual building up of the message of Islam.

## The Satanic Verses

The so-called "satanic verses" have also caused much misinterpretation in the West, fuelling the myth that the Quran is not a miracle—with the claim that certain verses were rigged by Muhammad. The satanic verses refer to an incident in the life of the Prophet in 619 when specific verses were allegedly spoken by Muhammad as part of the Quran, and then withdrawn on the grounds that Satan had sent them and deceived the Prophet into thinking that they had come from God. This incident is described by Ibn Ishaq (d. 768) in the first biography of the Prophet, and forms a subplot of the notorious novel by Salman Rushdie that was first published in 1988. The alleged verses allowed for prayers of intercession to be made to three Meccan goddesses: al-Lat, Manat, and al-Uzza—a major violation of the Islamic principle of monotheism.

The phrase that Arab historians and later Muslims used to describe this overblown incident, however, was the *gharaniq* (or "high-flying birds") verses since the phrase "satanic verses" was unknown to early Muslims. The phrase was actually coined by Western academics specializing in studying Islam and Middle Eastern culture, most notably Sir William Muir (d. 1905).

The title of the novel by Salman Rushdie refers to the incident which, according to Muslim scholars, is more fiction than fact. The satanic verses translate into English as "These are like high-flying birds whose intercession is to be hoped for."[9] The verses comprising the previous sentence are said to have been added to the initial fifty-third chapter of the Quran titled "The Star" in order to acknowledge the validity of the three goddesses al-Lat, Manat, and al-Uzza, and to appease the polytheist tribes of Mecca. The tradition goes on to say that the disputed verses were later withdrawn and denounced as inaccurate, and were replaced by the two modified verses which appear in the Quran as follows: "*But have you seen the goddesses al-Lat and al-Uzza, and the other one, Manat the third?*"[10] The historicity of the incident is disputed by many of the early Muslim historians, especially Ibn Ishaq who is considered an authority on the life of the Prophet.

Unfortunately, most Western commentators on the Quran have accepted this story of Muhammad's alleged momentary acceptance of the verses, while the vast majority of Muslim scholars have repudiated it. The prevailing Muslim view of the incident is that it is a fabrication created by the unbelievers of Mecca in the early days of Islam, and that afterwards the story had captivated the attention of Western orientalists who simply took it as true and repeated it *ad nauseam*.

The main argument against the authenticity of the so-called satanic verses is that its incoherence is evident with the least scrutiny. It basically contradicts the infallibility of every prophet, whether Moses, Jesus, or Muhammad, in conveying the message of his Lord. In other words, since Muslims believe that Muhammad faithfully and accurately reported all of God's words via Gabriel, the conclusion is that this bizarre story of Satan putting words into the Prophet's mouth is a fabrication and a forgery, authored by the enemies of Islam following the death of the Prophet.

## THE INTRINSIC BEAUTY OF THE QURAN

One of the common traits among the three divine faiths is that they were revealed in the Middle East in broadly similar languages: Judaism in Hebrew, Christianity in Aramaic, and Islam in Arabic, which itself is a derivative of both Hebrew and Aramaic. Seventh-century Arabia was a predominantly oral culture with the memorization of high poetry being the ultimate prize, with every tribe aspiring to create the most eloquent and elevated form of poetry as a way to impress and to prove the tribe's sophistication and superiority. Ukaz, a small market town not far from Mecca, would play host to an annual poetry festival where the craft of the poets (*al-shuaraa*) would be exhibited with great pride. Among the most famous poets of the pre-Islamic era were Imru al-Qays and Zuhayr ibn abi Sulma. Their work is both beautiful and intensely subjective, but not as soothing and stimulating to the soul as the Quran. The Quran is such a literary masterwork of Arabic prose and poetry that many of the first believers were converted by its sheer beauty, which resonated with their deepest fears and aspirations, slicing through their intellectual preconceptions in the manner of supreme art, and inspiring them at a level more deep than the intellectual, to alter their whole way of life.[11]

Muslims believe that the Quran is the only miracle of the Prophet Muhammad and that it is the last revealed word of God to humanity. The primary source of each Muslim's faith, moral compass, and practice, it deals with all the subjects concerning humans: law, wisdom, doctrine, marriage, worship, transactions, and the hereafter. However, one of its underlying themes is the direct relationship between God and His creations. The Quran also provides guidelines and teachings for the pursuit of happiness, a just and egalitarian society, proper human conduct, and an equitable economic system, calling people to worship the one and only God and to live their lives according to this sacred belief.

There is no doubt that when translated into other languages the Quran loses a lot of its intrinsic brilliance, hypnotic allure, and literary beauty. The same probably applies to the Torah and the verses of Jesus in the New Testament that were originally conveyed in Hebrew and Aramaic, respectively. Therefore, to simply judge the Quran in English, French, or German, for instance, is doing it great injustice (that's why all Muslims are encouraged to learn classical Arabic). When read in Arabic, there are so many verses that are breathtaking, leaving the reader in awe and with a unique feeling that its words could not have been invented by a human being, let alone an illiterate man who lived nearly 1,400 years ago. There have been many times when I read verses in the Quran that made my whole body shiver. These are some of these verses:

*God is the light*
*of the heavens and the earth.*
*The likeness of divine light*
*that is as of a niche with a lamp inside;*
*the lamp is in a glass;*
*the glass is as if a shining star,*
*lit from a blessed olive tree,*
*neither of the east nor of the west,*
*its oil nearly luminous*
*even without fire touching it.*
*Light upon light;*
*God guides whomever God wills*
*to divine light;*

*God gives people signs,*
*and God is knowing of everything.*[12]

*When the sun is rolled up*
*and when the stars fall lusterless*
*and when the mountains are blown away*
*and when the pregnant camels are neglected*
*and when the wild beasts are herded*
*and when the oceans are flooded*
*and when the souls are matched*
*and when the infant girl who was buried alive is asked*
*for what offense she was killed:*
*And when the pages are opened,*
*and when the sky is stripped*
*and when the blaze is fired up*
*and when the garden is drawn near*
*each soul will know*
*what it has brought about.*
*Yes, I swear by the planets that recede,*
*run, and disappear,*
*and the night as it darkens*
*and the dawn as it breaks*
*that these are the words of a noble messenger.*[13]

The Quran is viewed by Muslims as the literal word of God, a living miracle of the Prophet and a timeless gift from Muhammad to *all* of humanity, one that has no expiration date. It is a close companion in hardship and happiness—an eternal spirit enveloping its reader with the serenity and divinity of its rhythmic words.

Muslims believe that the Quran is a miracle for several reasons. Above all, it has been historically authenticated and verified in the Quran that Muhammad could not read or write. So for someone who was illiterate to be able to produce such a complex volume of literary beauty, social laws, scientific facts, and morality is in itself miraculous.

Revealed over the course of twenty-two years, and often under extremely stressful conditions, the Quran maintains its constant tone and literary style. That is, over the course of more than two decades, a writer's personality would normally evolve and change, and so would his or her style of oral expression. That is not the case with the Quran, the constant prose and diction of which are completely different from the sayings of the Prophet. In my view, this is proof that the Quran was not made up by Muhammad, as many Western critics claim. It demonstrates that Muhammad was a receiver of a stream of messages revealed to him from a realm of timeless existence.

In terms of scientific facts, the Quran, for example, speaks about the successive stages of human embryonic development:

> *We created the human being*
> *from an extract of earth,*
> *then placed it as a drop*
> *in a secure repository;*
> *then We made the drop a clot,*
> *then we made the clot a lump of flesh,*
> *then We made the flesh bones,*
> *then We clothed the bones with flesh,*
> *and then We produced another creature from it.*[14]

The Prophet also once said, "If forty days have passed over the embryo, God sends an angel to it, who shapes and creates its hearing, vision, skin, flesh, and bones."[15] Other scientific facts mentioned in the Quran include the expansion of the universe, the formation of seas and clouds, the human brain's cerebrum, and the slightly oval shape of the earth.[16]

Our universe is a beautiful place. There are many hidden structures and complicated mechanisms at play that we're just beginning to figure out. Mathematics is the true magic underlying the workings of our universe, and as humans we feel compelled to discover as much of this magic as we can. God describes the structure of the Quran when He conveys that it's a numerically coded book (*kitabun marqoum*), which indicates that in addition to its primary role as a moral guide for a better way of life, it has mysterious numerical symmetries to prove its divine origin.[17] For example, the sacred scripture of Islam has a remarkable equilibrium of words, some of which are as follows:[18]

| | |
|---|---|
| The word meaning "world of this life" in Arabic (and its derivatives) is mentioned 115 times. | The word "hereafter" in Arabic (and its derivatives) is mentioned 115 times. |
| The word "life" is repeated 145 times. | The word "death" is repeated 145 times. |
| "Righteous deeds" 167 times. | "Evil deeds" 167 times. |
| "Angels" 88 times. | "Demons" 88 times. |
| "Hot" 4 times. | "Cold" 4 times. |
| "Summer" 1 time. | "Winter" 1 time. |

The underlying message of this equilibrium of words in the Quran could be that God is conveying the vital concept of balance—all the way from the complex mechanics of the universe to the ways that we go about our daily lives. To achieve a meaningful way of life and to attain happiness, God is telling us that balance and moderation are vital—that extremism is self-defeating.

## A BOOK OF MERCY AND TRANQUILITY

While the Muslim stance is often falsely perceived as being authoritarian and punitive, the Quran is filled with gentle attributes such as providence, love, and tenderheartedness. Those who claim that the Quran is a book of hate and violence need to know that the word "kill" (and its derivatives, such as "killed" and "killing") is actually mentioned 172 times, or only 0.2 percent of the Quran's total 77,701 words. In turn, the word "love" and the word "mercy" (and their derivatives, such as "loving" and "merciful") can be counted 437 times. Furthermore, of God's ninety-nine names that are mentioned in the Quran, twenty-three of them directly describe Him as loving, forgiving, and merciful.[19] Far from being a book of hate and violence, the Quran is a medium that grants its readers tranquility and inner peace:

*O tranquil soul,*
*"return to your Creator, pleased and accepted:*
*Enter the company of My worshippers;*
*enter peacefully into My paradise."* [20]

## CONCLUSION

The sacred scripture of Islam is an eternal book that was created to help Muslims live a meaningful and productive life, enabling them to overcome their innermost anxieties and temptations. I have read the Quran in its entirety in Arabic only once, but it took me six months. That's because when I read it, I also studied the interpretations of each verse and the specific purpose and timing of each revelation.[21] In doing so, I was humbled by its subtle prose, which is succinct, with stippled poetic touches that awaken breathtaking evocations.

The Quran is a vast ocean—full of mystery, deep darkness, beauty, and rays of bright sunlight. Many of its 6,236 verses can be understood in various ways because the Prophet was instructed by God not to explain the meaning of any of the verses during his lifetime. It is presented in such a way that every time a Muslim is exposed to the text, the words could mean something different—something new. God wanted the Quran to be an "elastic text," most of its verses to be interpreted flexibly during different eras, with each period's own prevailing knowledge, logic, and common sense, with major significance to be placed on *when* and *why* each verse was originally revealed. Therefore, it's vital to distinguish between two important categories of verses: those tied to the specific context of seventh-century Arabia, and those that are timeless and open to flexible interpretation.

The myth that the Quran is not a miracle will continue for many centuries to come, with the skeptics claiming that it's a book of hate, violence, and the oppression of women. However, I suspect that those who believe that it's not the word of God believe so because they don't read its verses in their contextual frame. That is, they don't make an effort to understand the purpose and implied meaning of its verses. The great irony here is that the first word revealed to humanity through the Prophet Muhammad was, in fact, "Read!"

Too many times Western critics lazily quote a single verse and then take it completely out of context, ignoring the underlying characteristic of the Quran—that its verses are harmoniously interwoven and built upon one another in such a way that ultimately renders the book complete. Sure, there are verses and words that we still don't fully understand, but their secrets shall be gradually unraveled to Muslims and non-Muslims alike until the end of time:

> *If you are in doubt of what We have revealed...*
> *then try to bring a chapter like it...*
> *It is God who has revealed*
> *the Book to you,*
> *including precise signs,*
> *which are the matrix of the Book,*
> *and others that are ambiguous.*[22]
> *We will show them Our signs*
> *throughout the regions of the earth*
> *and in themselves,*
> *until it becomes clear to them*
> *that the Quran is the truth.*[23]

# MYTH THREE:

## The Prophet Muhammad Basked
## in Sensual Delight

I can't deny that when I first learned that the Prophet Muhammad had a total of twelve wives, I was quite shocked. But I was shocked because I initially took this sociological and multilayered issue superficially, benchmarking it against modern society's matrimonial practices. After further research, I realized that something was wrong with the rumors, false allegations, and preconceived opinions surrounding the twelve marriages of Muhammad. Something was not right, because it has been historically authenticated that when the Prophet was a teenager and in his twenties, he avoided the temptations of women and hedonism that were rampant in Mecca. Muhammad was so well-mannered, trustworthy, and caring of others that he was known as *al-Ameen*, the honest one. Muhammad preferred to be alone, or to watch his goats and sheep (before becoming a successful merchant, he was a shepherd boy) while his friends and relatives indulged in rampant prostitution, gambling, and excessive drinking. He would isolate himself from Mecca's decadent society for weeks on end, fasting and contemplating how the raging vices of humanity must be changed. Sensual delight was the last thing on his mind.

### THE ERA OF DARK IGNORANCE *(al-Jahiliyya)*

It's paramount to put into context the era and cultural milieu in which Muhammad lived some 1,400 years ago. At the time of the Prophet, tribal Arabia was a hopeless situation—a terrible and brutal place plagued with wars, political conflict, and barbarism. It was also a cutthroat capitalist culture that thrived on insatiable lust and corruption. The most powerful men of Mecca, who were brilliant at trade, often had numerous wives whom they would divorce without thinking twice. As a consequence, they had numerous children, but preferred males. The wealthy men would bury their infant daughters alive, claiming that females brought dishonor to tribes. It was a grotesque way of showing their wives that only males were worthy of living to enhance the prestige of their tribes. This is why the era is called *al-Jahiliyya* by Arab historians, or the era of dark ignorance. This is also why God chose a messenger to penetrate human society at this specific place and time to remind people of the self-destruction that can stem from incessant sin and moral bankruptcy.

During al-Jahiliyya, it was common to marry a woman soon after her husband died; otherwise she would have no other means of survival, especially if she had numerous children to sustain. At the time of Muhammad, Arabia was an ultra-male-dominated society, with its socioeconomic fabric derived directly from the primitive traditions of Bedouin tribes and the greedy merchants of Mecca. It was also common to marry and abuse orphaned females, to marry for the sole purpose of bringing rival tribes together, or to facilitate a large trade deal between families. Women were treated as leased property, and had absolutely no rights of inheritance or freedom of choice.

Another widespread practice at the time was to engage and marry women at a young age. At times, and for the sake of protecting an unborn baby from being buried alive if it turned out to be a girl, pregnant mothers would announce that, "Whatever baby is in this womb shall marry whatever baby is in that womb," desperately hoping that the two would turn out to be of the opposite sex so that the announced engagement could actually happen. In other words, boys and girls were sometimes engaged before they were even born.

There was also a high rate of infant mortality because of the absence of sophisticated medicine. Therefore, it was purely a numbers game: marry young and have as many children as possible with the hope that some might survive. Lifespan was another critical factor. With no effective medical care whatsoever, coupled with rampant tribal wars and murder, the average lifetime of people in Arabia was probably no more than fifty-five at the time. The Prophet himself lost all his three sons, al-Qasem, Abdullah, and Abraham, to disease before they reached the age of one, although Muslims believe that it was God's will for Muhammad to not have any male heirs so that an Islamic "kingdom" of sorts wouldn't evolve.

### THE WIVES OF THE PROPHET

Muhammad was twenty-five when he married his first wife, Khadija, who was fifteen years older than he and had been married twice before. She remained his loyal wife for twenty-eight years until she died. Most importantly, he did *not* marry any other woman during that period of his life, which was remarkable for that era. This tells us that between the ages of twenty-five and fifty-three, the peak years of male libido and sexual activity, Muhammad was not eagerly seeking sensual delight. He was always faithful to Khadija's memory, so much that this loyalty created jealousy among some of his other wives whom he married in later years. As such, how could a man who was more than fifty years old suddenly change and become a slave to lust when he had every opportunity as a young man to succumb to his sensual desires, as the other men of Mecca did? The Prophet's kind nature, well-balanced character, and humble way of life before his prophethood are proof that he was neither a lustful nor a pleasure-seeking man.

In an attempt to debunk the notorious myth that the Prophet basked in sensual delight, the following table lays out the facts about Muhammad's twelve wives, along with the specific reasons for each of his marriages. The Prophet did not divorce any of his spouses, which was extremely uncommon at the time. Most of his wives were widows whom he married for humane reasons, not for sexual desires on his part. In fact, most of his spouses were a burden on him, given their jealousy of one another. An additional point to highlight is that he had children with only two of his twelve wives.

Some other prophets who practiced polygamy were Abraham, David, and Solomon. Abraham had three wives (Sarah, Hagar, and Keturah), and the Bible indicates that Abraham also had concubines and had children with them. It has been recorded that David had eight wives who are named in the Bible, but there were numerous other spouses who were not named, while Solomon had some seven hundred wives and three hundred concubines. Does this imply that these prophets were lustful men? To the contrary, the practice of polygamy during their times was widely accepted and practiced for both social and political reasons. (As a reminder to the reader, Islam permits men to marry up to four wives based on strict conditions that encompass treating them equally in *all* aspects of daily life, whether financial, emotional, or social).

## THE WIVES OF THE PROPHET[1]

| NAME | DURATION OF MARRIAGE* | WIFE'S AGE AT MARRIAGE | NUMBER OF CHILDREN WITH THE PROPHET | REASON OF MARRIAGE/COMMENTS |
|---|---|---|---|---|
| 1. Khadija | 28 years | 40 | 4 girls (Zeynab, Ruqayya, Um Kulthoum, and Fatima); and 2 boys (al-Qasem and Abdullah). | Khadija was the one who proposed to the Prophet. She was attracted to Muhammad because of his honesty as a merchant. Muhammad did not marry another woman during Khadija's lifetime. The Prophet was in his prime (25) when he married her. |
| 2. Sawda | 14 years | 65 | None | To take care of his family after Khadija died. Sawda was an older widow of no beauty or wealth. This marriage served as an example to marry those women in need of financial support after the death of their husbands. |
| 3. Aisha | 11 years | 15** | None | To strengthen the Prophet's ties with his first aide, Abou Bakr, Aisha's father; to educate and train her for the purposes of Islam; and to utilize her capabilities for the sake of spreading Islam. Aisha was the only virgin among all the Prophet's wives. Among all his wives, Muhammad loved Aisha the most. |

| | | | | |
|---|---|---|---|---|
| 4. Hafsa | 8 years | 21 | None | To strengthen the Prophet's ties with his second aide, Omar (Hafsa's father). Muhammad also married Hafsa to sustain her after her husband was killed in war. She's believed to be the only wife who had the original version of the Quran in its written format, given to her by Omar. Some scholars believe that Aisha had a second copy as well. |
| 5. Zeynab bint Khuzayma | 8 months | 29 | None | To sustain her after her husband was killed in war. She died quite young from illness. |
| 6. Um Salama Hind | 7 years | 34 | None | To strengthen the Prophet's ties with her father's large Meccan tribe, the Makhzum, and to sustain her after her husband was killed in war. |
| 7. Zeynab bint Jahsh | 6 years | 35 | None | Her first husband was Zaid ibn Haritha, who was raised by the Prophet as his only adopted son. It is only after Zaid divorced Zeynab that the Prophet married her. |
| 8. Juwayriyya | 6 years | 21 | None | To free her from slavery. She was the first Jew the Prophet married. |

| Name | | Age | Children | |
|---|---|---|---|---|
| 9. Safiyya | 4 years | 17 | None | To free her from slavery. She was the second Jew the Prophet married. The marriage to Safiyya had a political significance as well, as it helped to reduce hostilities and cement alliances with certain Jewish tribes in Medina. |
| 10. Ramla | 4 years | 37 | None | To improve relations with her father, Abou Sufyan ibn Harb, the leader of Mecca and the Prophet's worst enemy. He also married Ramla to sustain her after her husband was killed in Abyssinia. Another name used for Ramla is Um Habiba. |
| 11. Maymoona | 4 years | 25 | None | To sustain her after she was divorced from her second husband. Her real name was Barra, but Muhammad liked to call her Maymoona, which means "blessed." |
| 12. Maria | 4 years | 17 | 1 boy (Abraham) | Maria was the third slave that the Prophet married. He had a son with her to confirm the rights of bondwomen to get married and to enjoy an honorable life. She was the only Christian the Prophet married. This marriage also created a significant political alliance with the ruler of Egypt, al-Muqawqus. Muhammad was 58 when he wedded Maria. |
| Average Age | | 30 | | |

*The most number of wives, or overlapping marriages, that the Prophet had at any one time was ten, which must have been a challenging task for him, as evidenced by several hadith.

**See the more detailed information on Aisha's age upon marriage, discussed in the text that follows.

### Aisha

Of the Prophet's twelve wives, there is one that has created significant controversy in the West, leading to the false claim that Muhammad was a womanizer and, even worse, a pedophile. This wife is Aisha, the Prophet's third bride and Abou Bakr's daughter, and the controversy surrounding Aisha is her age when she was married. Muslims believe that the Prophet didn't marry Aisha out of his own sensual desires; rather, it was driven initially by a divine inspiration as narrated in the following oral tradition: "The Prophet said to Aisha, 'You have been shown to me twice in a dream. I saw you portrayed on a piece of cloth and someone said [to me], 'This is your wife.' When I uncovered the image, I saw that it was yours. I said, 'If this is from God, it will be done.'"[2]

With the help of a prophetic eye, Muhammad could see that the young Aisha was going to be a highly intelligent and charismatic woman when she grew up. Eager to pass his sayings and instructions to Muslims and non-Muslims through her, the Prophet brought Aisha into his house so that he could bring her up in accordance with his long-term religious goals.

Aisha, who had a formidable memory and was an excellent public speaker, became one of the greatest female scholars of Islam, setting an example for future generations of Muslim women. Aisha is sometimes described as the most knowledgeable about Islam after the Prophet himself, even by his male companions. After the Prophet died, many of his companions would come to Aisha to seek the deep knowledge that only she had and that only she was privy to. Her example of being highly regarded, especially among Muslim men, plays an important role in removing the uncertainties regarding women as being inferior to men in aspects of Islamic teachings, or false notions hindering women from earning a high status in Muslim society. Aisha, who is often referred to as the "Mother of the Believers," died in 678, some forty-six years after the Prophet, which enabled her to fulfill her mission as a medium of Islamic teachings and scholarship. Muslims also believe that Muhammad's marriage to Aisha took place to strengthen the ties between himself and her father, his closest companion, Abou Bakr, as was widely practiced among the tribes of Arabia at the time.

Sadly, many Western critics choose the lowest age of marriage for Aisha. Not only that, but they tend to go out of their way to try to prove that Muhammad was a pedophile because of the confusion surrounding Aisha's age. These critics don't explain the full context and purpose of her marriage to the Prophet. The numerous conflicting reports about Aisha's age when married have been the cornerstone of the formation of the Western myth that Muhammad lived as an Arabian sultan in lavish palaces with his imperial harem. It should not be forgotten that factors such as similar practices at the time contribute to this hugely warped view. As noted earlier, we should evaluate this myth according to the cultural context of the relevant time. Otherwise, if we were to attempt to evaluate the historical events of al-Jahiliyya within today's social parameters, we are bound to make mistakes.

During the time of the Prophet, there was no year-counting as we have now (i.e., 2011). If we asked people of his time, "When was Muhammad born?" they wouldn't simply say, "around 570 CE." Rather, they would say, "He was born in the Year of the Elephant." According to Muslim historians, Abraha, the governor of Yemen—then a province of the Christian Kingdom of Aksum (present-day Ethiopia)—attempted to destroy the Kaaba in Mecca with an army that included elephants. Because it was customary to name a year after a major event, that year became known as the Year of the Elephant, which was also the year in which Muhammad is believed to have been born (570).

As background, Islamic years are called *hijri* because the first year was the one during which the hijra (the emigration of Muhammad from Mecca to Medina) took place. It is well known that the hijra occurred fifty-two years after the Year of the Elephant (or in 622), and it has been recorded that Abou Bakr's first daughter, Asma, was born twenty-seven years before the hijra (or in 595).[3] It has also been recorded by Muslim scholars that the age difference between Aisha and her sister Asma was ten years.[4] According to this information, Aisha's year of birth was 605 (595 + 10 = 605), and her age at the time of the hijra was, therefore, seventeen (622 - 605 = 17). Since her marriage is known to have taken place two years after the hijra, this indicates that Aisha was approximately nineteen when Muhammad became her husband.

In addition, it is known that Aisha was engaged to a man named Jober ibn Oday before her engagement to the Prophet.[5] This engagement took place approximately one year before Muhammad officially started preaching his message, or around the year 611, because Muslim scholars note that Jober wasn't aware of Islam. Aisha's father, Abou Bakr, broke her engagement with Jober because he didn't convert to Islam after it began to gradually circulate as a new religion in Mecca in 612; therefore, the breakup probably took place around 613, a year after Islam was out in the open. By applying the tradition of the time of women getting engaged at a young age, let's assume that Aisha was about six when she got engaged to Jober, and eight years old when Abou Bakr broke her engagement to Jober in 613. This means that she could have been born in 605 (613 - 8 = 605). Again, since Muhammad and Aisha got married two years after the hijra, which occurred in 622, this places their marriage in the year 624. According to this information, Aisha was nineteen years old when she married the Prophet (624 - 605 = 19).

On the other hand, al-Bukhari (d. 870), one of the major collectors of the sayings, actions, and recordings (hadith) pertaining to the life of the Prophet, relayed that Aisha was nine years old when she became betrothed to Muhammad, but did not consummate her marriage to the Prophet until after reaching puberty, which is when every girl in Arabia, without exception, became eligible for marriage.[6] Therefore, based on all these conflicting dates, it is safe to say that the exact age of Aisha when she married Muhammad is basically unknown.

It has been reported that al-Bukhari initially researched and analyzed some 600,000 hadith of the Prophet, but painstakingly filtered them down to only 2,980 (or 0.5 percent of the total) as being, in his judgment, authentic. In basic terms, the compiled hadith by al-Bukhari are "as good as it gets." When compared to the other compilers of Muhammad's sayings, al-Bukhari is the most reliable source because he was so diligent and applied such scrutiny in his research and methodology. Nonetheless, we must be mindful that al-Bukhari was born nearly 180 years after the death of the Prophet, meaning there is a probability of human error affecting the relaying of his filtered hadith. Whether this human error factor comprises a 1 percent deviation or a 10 percent deviation from what Muhammad actually said is something we'll never know.

According to the analysis presented above, there is little doubt that Aisha was young when she married Muhammad, but there is reliable support for her being older than the assumed nine years relayed by al-Bukhari. All of the above arguments are based on the hypothesis that—as reported by the original sources—the *age* at which Aisha was married is wrong, while the *year* when she married is correct. That is, all the sources agree that she was married in the year 624, but are inconsistent as to the date of Aisha's birth.

A balanced approach, and without fluffing the available data, is to take the average of the three ages extrapolated from the three aforementioned sources: nineteen years old, as benchmarked by Aisha's age in relation to her sister, Asma; nineteen years old, according to the sequence of dates in terms of her first engagement to Jober ibn Oday; and nine years old, as related by al-Bukhari. This simple approach results in an average age for Aisha of about fifteen when she married the Prophet.

## MUHAMMAD: A HUMBLE MAN

Muhammad was a humble man who lived modestly, forbidding himself the good food, fancy clothing, monumental palaces, and dictatorial authority that typically came with positions of leadership in seventh-century Arabia. Muhammad was not only a prophet, father, and husband, but also a brilliant statesman and military strategist, given the bellicose sociopolitical environment in which he lived. In his basic home in Medina, the Prophet slept on the floor on a mattress made of leather stuffed with the fibers of date palm trees. He had a simple diet comprised mainly of dates, bread, camel milk, and water. He often helped out with the housework, such as milking his goat, sewing clothes, and repairing his shoes. Muhammad had also accustomed his wives, who lived in separate quarters, to dialogue with him; he listened to their advice, and the wives debated and even argued with him. Muhammad's wives, however, clearly distinguished his role as a prophet from his role as a husband. He did not allow his wives to use his status as a prophet and highly influential leader to obtain special treatment in public or to attain material wealth. When he died, he left neither money nor material possessions for his family, except his white riding mule and a piece of land which they gave to charity.[7]

At the outset of a long and painful era of torture, suffering, and persecution of Muhammad and his followers that took place in Mecca between 612 and 622, and long before there was any real prospect of success for Islam, he received a lucrative offer. Sensing the threat that Muhammad could eventually pose, the polytheist leader Otba and his envoy came to the Prophet saying: "If you want money, we will collect enough money for you so that you will be the richest one of us. If you want leadership, we will take you as our leader and never decide on any matter without your approval. If you want a kingdom, we will crown you as king."[8]

However, one concession was required of the Prophet in return for their tempting offer—that Muhammad must permanently give up calling people to Islam and worshipping God. The Prophet refused Otba's offer, and reiterated his cause by saying: "I swear by God that even if they put the sun in my right hand and the moon in my left, and in return demand of me to quit the pursuance of my divine aim, I will never do what they want me to. I am determined to carry on my duty toward God to the very last moment of my life."[9]

Muhammad taught love and mercy to all of God's creations. There are many reports of his love for cats, for example. It has been recorded that there was a woman who locked up a cat, refusing to feed it and not releasing it so that the cat could somehow feed itself. In response, the Prophet said that her punishment on the day of judgment will be torture. Muhammad's favorite cat was called Muezza, and there is a widely circulated story about Muezza that recounts when a call to prayer was given, and as Muhammad went to put on one of his robes, he found his cat sleeping on one of the robe's sleeves. Instead of disturbing the cat, he cut off the sleeve and let Muezza sleep.[10] Are these the characteristics of a power-hungry, self-centered, or lustful man, as many Western observers proclaim?

Muhammad's followers loved, respected, and trusted him to the utmost degree. Yet the Prophet would continuously emphasize that deification should be directed only to God and not to him personally. Anas ibn Malik (d. 709), one of Muhammad's companions, said that there was no person whom they loved more than the Prophet, yet when he entered into a room they would never stand up for him as other people did with their revered leaders, because Muhammad disliked that superficial gesture.[11] Would his companions have loved and respected him if he was a ruthless man, as is often claimed in the West?

Numerous passages in the Quran prohibit idolatry and the worshipping of statues or paintings. As such, images and drawings of the Prophet are forbidden in Islam. However, several of his companions gave a detailed description of Muhammad's persona, granting us a glance at this humble man who completely changed the course of world history in twenty-two years:

"When he addressed a person, the Prophet turned his whole body toward that person and gave his full attention... He was most generous, truthful, and kind-hearted. Any person who saw him would become awe-inspired...The Prophet had such a great personality and such dignity that the person who saw him for the first time would be overcome with a feeling of profound respect...I have not seen anyone like Muhammad, neither before nor after him."[12]

### MUHAMMAD AND THE FEMALE GENDER

Through his egalitarian reforms, Muhammad dramatically changed the status of women in ultra-male-dominated Arabia and his social reform movement quickly transformed into a universal religious ideology. In the historical context of his time, the Prophet can be seen as a figure that promoted women's rights and improved their status considerably. Specifically, he instituted women's rights of property ownership, inheritance, education, and divorce, and gave them basic safeguards in society, which are too complex to be discussed here.

Muhammad would repeatedly ask for and follow the advice of his wives, even in military matters. He refused that women be confined to their homes and asked them to attend worship at the mosque alongside men. It was actually Omar—the second caliph of Islam—who instituted segregated prayers in Islam and, in direct violation of Muhammad's practice, forced women to be taught by male religious clerics. He banned the Prophet's widows to travel to Mecca to perform the hajj, probably because he felt that he had to protect them. Although Omar was a highly dignified and pious man, he also instituted a series of harsh penal ordinances aimed primarily at women, namely the stoning to death of adulterers. (As will be discussed in chapter 9, this is a punishment which has absolutely no foundation whatsoever in the Quran).

There is no doubt that Muhammad was a man who had the deepest respect for the female gender, and genuinely wanted them to succeed and be an integral part of society. Sadly, after the Prophet's death, many of his revolutionary ideas were dampened by men who were more interested in regaining the financial and social dominance that Muhammad's reforms had taken from them.

## CONCLUSION

A levelheaded way to approach the myth that the Prophet was a womanizer who basked in sensual delight is to ask, "Could Muhammad—the man of supreme virtue who communicated God's message of mercy to all humanity, the man who was so kind and humble—have been a pedophile?" In common usage, the term "pedophile" refers to any adult who is sexually attracted to children or who sexually abuses a child. Moreover, a man who's a pedophile is mentally ill and has no moral compass. In law enforcement in the United States, the term is generally used to describe those accused or convicted of the senseless sexual abuse of a minor, including both prepubescent children and adolescent minors younger than the local age of consent.[13] It should be noted that in the US, early and prolific marriages were common in the eighteenth century when the average age of first marriages for all American women was only twenty. In some parts of the country, it was as low as thirteen.[14] Does this indicate that American men at the time were pedophiles? Of course not; it was simply common social practice.

By using common sense and logic in relation to the information that we have today about Muhammad's character and the cultural context of Arabia during al-Jahiliyya, coupled with the specific reasons behind each of the Prophet's twelve marriages that took place about 1,400 years ago, we can deduct that Muhammad was a man who had the highest respect for women. If Aisha, for the sake of argument, was sexually abused by the Prophet when she was nine, as Western critics advertise, would she have stayed with the Prophet to see him take his last breaths on his deathbed? Would she have remained loyal to the cause of Islam for the rest of her life?

The relationship between Aisha and the Prophet was beyond the trivia of temporal sex and sensual delight. It was more about getting the universal message of Islam out to the world via a highly intelligent, strong-willed young woman. This is what Muhammad had in mind when he married Aisha, so that humanity could have a chance to benefit from a balanced way of life that's built upon the teachings of Abraham, Moses, and Jesus, and further amplified by the Prophet—a divine message that conveys social justice, equality, and, above all, the respect of women's rights.[15]

# MYTH FOUR:

**Women Have No Rights in Islam**

Islam is an egalitarian religion, and the Muslim faith's underlying attitude toward women's rights is crystallized in 3:195 of the Quran:

> *And their Lord answered them:*
> *"I am never unmindful of the work*
> *of a worker among you, male or female.*
> *You are equal to one another."*

The relatively few cases of ill treatment that women receive in the Muslim world today are primarily due to local cultures, without any basis in the faith of Islam itself. Crude practices such as forced marriage, female circumcision, and restricted movement directly contradict Islamic law (sharia) governing family behavior and personal freedom. These primitive practices are a result of the continuation of male-dominated, Bedouin-oriented traditions that were in existence *prior* to Islam.

Before Islam was introduced in Arabia some 1,400 years ago, women were treated as mere material possessions with no rights whatsoever. After the spread of Islam, the status of women improved dramatically, due largely to the Prophet's revolutionary call for the freedom and respect of all women. During his lifetime, Muslim women participated in commerce, political debates, battles, and joint prayer. Accordingly, Islam granted women rights many centuries before Western women were given any such benefits. It is, therefore, essential to differentiate between the laws of Islam, which protect the respect and safety of women, and the pre-Islamic customs which have, in some rare cases, stubbornly prevailed, preventing women from being educated or taking a lead role in society, because of ignorance and male-serving thinking.

In addition to the negativity associated with primitive practices, the myth that women have no rights in Islam is related to the misunderstandings surrounding the following four teachings of Islamic law:[1]

1. Women are encouraged to dress in a way that conveys modesty.
2. Men can marry up to four wives, only if their just treatment is guaranteed.
3. A man's share of inheritance is greater than that of a woman's.
4. A woman's testimony in court is not considered equal to that of a man.

## THE VEIL

The warped image of the veiled Muslim woman as the sheltered, passive sexual object of her husband has been clouding Western minds for centuries. Every country has its distinct character and way of life, with its own traditional food, architecture, and attire that celebrate its people's culture and beliefs. In a similar vein, Muslim women have the right to choose to be proud of their religious heritage, which may be outwardly reflected in their attire.

Many Muslims believe that the Quran and the collected traditions of the life of the Prophet (hadith and sunna) require both men and women to dress and behave decently and modestly in public. The attire that Islam asks of a Muslim woman is that she appears in a decent and respectable manner in order to protect her from any unpleasant remarks, humiliating leering, or from being harassed by uncontrolled men. To that end, the Muslim attire for women is intended to safeguard their honor and dignity, and is not in any way intended to be a tool of female oppression, as is often assumed in the West.

The origins of the veil (or headscarf) in Islam are several. The custom of veiling is believed to have originated from the Bedouin tribes of pre-Islamic Arabia who, due to the frequent sandstorms and scorching sunlight, had to cover their heads. The customs of veiling and the seclusion of women in early Islam were also assimilated from the conquered Byzantine, Jewish, and Persian societies (around the year 640), and then later on were adopted as appropriate expressions of Islamic values related to female modesty and privacy. Moreover, the teachings related to modesty are attributed to the interpretation of several verses in the Quran.

The Prophet conducted all religious and civic affairs in the mosque adjacent to his house in Medina, which was quite small and had limited space for privacy. People from all walks of life were constantly coming in and out of his compound at all hours of the day and for all sorts of reasons, including consultations, meals, meetings, and prayers. When delegations from other tribes or regions came to speak with Muhammad, they would set up their tents for days inside the open courtyard a few feet from the areas in which his wives slept, perhaps making him feel a bit protective. New emigrants arriving in Medina would also stay within the mosque's walls for weeks until they found adequate housing. According to narrations by Anas ibn Malik and an authentic hadith relayed by al-Bukhari, by instituting seclusion and privacy, Muhammad was creating a respectful barrier and separation, or *hijab*, between his wives and this bustling community on their doorstep. Hence, the revelation of this verse in chapter 33 of the Quran:

> *...And when you ask the wives of the Prophet*
> *for something needed,*
> *ask them from behind a screen (hijab):*
> *that is purer for your hearts*
> *and their hearts.*[2]

Here, the word "screen" is translated from the Arabic word "hijab," a term that's widely (and somewhat inaccurately) used today to describe the traditional head cover for women. In addition to "screen," the hijab can be interpreted as "curtain," "drape," "partition," and/or "divider." The classical Arabic word for a veil, as interpreted from the Quran, is actually *khimar,* and not hijab. The word hijab is mentioned seven times in the Quran, always in the context of a separating barrier or physical partition. For example, in 42:51: "*It is not possible for a human being that God should speak to him but by inspiration or from behind a partition (hijab).*"

The precise word that's used in the following verse is *khumurihinna,* which is translated as "coverings." It is the plural of the word "khimar" in the feminine tense, and is understood to mean a woman's headscarf or a piece of cloth with which a woman covers her head. The Muslim scholar Raghib al-Isfahani (d. 1109) explained the pertinent terminology by saying, "The root meaning of the word 'khimar' is to cover, and the khimar, therefore, is a cover or veil, but it has become synonymous with the hijab with which a woman covers her head." In addition, according to the ancient Arabic dictionary *Lisaan al-Arab,* (or *The Tongue of the Arabs*), the word "khimar" means and was used in the seventh century to refer to a piece of cloth that covers the head, commonly known today as the hijab.

> *And tell the believing women*
> *to lower their eyes and guard their privates*
> *and not to show their ornaments*
> *except the obvious ones,*
> *and to draw their coverings (khumurihinna)*
> *over their chests (jeubihinna)*
> *and not display their beauty*
> *except to their fathers and husbands.*[3]

At the time of the Prophet, the majority of women in Mecca and Medina were not veiled. They walked in public with light clothing due to the extremely hot weather conditions between the months of March and October. The veil was used at first as a sign to distinguish the high-status, free woman so that none would molest her, thinking that she was an available slave or a streetwalker who attracted unsavory attention. For that reason, the following verses were also revealed in relation to female attire:

> *O Prophet, tell your wives,*
> *your daughters, and the believing women*
> *to put on their outer garments (jalabibihinna);*
> *that is most convenient*
> *so they will be recognized*
> *and not molested.*
> *God is very forgiving, most merciful.*[4]
> *...And settle down in your homes,*
> *and don't show off in public*
> *with dazzling clothing*
> *as was done in the former times of ignorance.*[5]

There are millions of highly commendable Muslim women worldwide who genuinely believe that wearing the veil is one of the ways to please God, showing their infinite love toward Him and adhering to His teachings with regard to female modesty and decency. Mother Teresa of India and Mary (Mother of Jesus) wore veils, while Christian nuns and Orthodox Jewish women today tend to wear similar attire. In Jerusalem and Manhattan at present, thousands of Jewish women freely express their religious identity through modest attire and "covering up." Hair covering among Jewish women can be traced to Jewish law. The Jewish scholar Moses Maimonides (d. 1204) is quoted in the Mishneh Torah as stating that the covering of a woman's hair is derived from the teachings of Moses and the Old Testament.

Unfortunately, the wearing of the veil is enforced in Afghanistan, and is currently imposed upon women in Iran and Saudi Arabia. These countries require that women not only cover their heads, but, in some cases, their faces as well, because in their outdated view, "The face of a woman is a provocation for men not related to them."[6] Countries such as Afghanistan, Iran, and Saudi Arabia insist that "covering up" by Muslim women who have reached puberty is obligatory, and is a commandment by God. However, it is important to realize that such all-covering attire predates Islam, and is part of the indigenous cultures of these societies.

An extreme form of covering up, which has absolutely nothing to do with Islam, is the *burqa*, an enveloping outer garment worn by women in some Islamic countries for the purpose of cloaking the entire body. The spooky-looking burqa, which is a current reflection of the religiously inspired misogyny of radical groups such as the Taliban, originated in what's known today as Afghanistan and northwest Pakistan, long before Islam arrived. Worn by both men and women, the burqa originally had two functions: Firstly, as a sort of mask for sandy and windy conditions. Secondly, the masking of the face and body was used for women when one tribe was being attacked by another. These raids often involved the kidnapping of women of child-bearing age. With all women hidden behind a burqa, and the home army fighting back, the chances of being kidnapped were reduced, as the women of child-bearing age could not be quickly distinguished from the young or the old. As such, women wore the burqa for safety and as protection from the brutal abuse by men.

When traveling in the Middle East and elsewhere, it's becoming more and more common to see women wearing a black burqa that may or may not only show their eyes (also known in Arabic as a *niqab*). This bizarre trend began when expatriates started to go and work in conservative countries such as Saudi Arabia in the early 1980s, returning to their home countries with an inaccurate understanding that the full covering with a burqa must be applied by all Muslim women. Burqa-style attire is not mentioned anywhere in the Quran. It has been blended into mainstream Islam based on old cultural traditions, and erroneously enforced upon women as a religious commandment. Islamic law does not command women to cover their faces with a niqab, or to wear gloves, as is sometimes practiced—all primitive customs that belong to certain societies for which Islam is in no way responsible.

The Prophet was known to despise black attire, preferring brighter colors, such as white and green, since black is the worst color to wear in the hot Arabian climate because it attracts heat and sunlight, and because it is a universal symbol of mourning. On the flip side, in the Gulf countries (Bahrain, Kuwait, Oman, Qatar, Saudi Arabia, and the UAE), most men today wear the traditional white *dishdasha* which is made of soft cotton and is comfortable and heat-resistant due to its reflective color. This traditional Arabian attire, which, similar to the niqab, has nothing to do with Islam, is a result of local customs being preserved over the centuries for the benefit of men.

Regrettably, the issue of the veil has taken on "larger-than-life" proportions in both Western and Muslim countries.

Muslim scholars believe that since the covering of the head is the most important function of a veil, they don't dispute that Muslim women are asked to cover their heads. The four major Sunni schools of thought (Hanafi, Shafii, Maliki, and Hanbali) believe that the entire body of a woman, except her face and hands, are part of her *awra*—the parts of a woman's body that should be covered during prayer and in public settings. As such, there is little doubt that Islamic law urges women to dress modestly, and a way to convey such modesty and piety is to wear a veil. In an effort to update the interpretations of the relevant Quranic verses, some Muslim scholars recommend that women wear clothing that is not tight on the body, revealing, or sexually arousing—modest forms of Western clothing such as long shirts and skirts.

On the other hand, there are some Muslims today who believe that a woman should have the right to choose to wear (or not to wear) the veil as she deems appropriate. They believe that if a woman chooses to wear the veil, she should be fully respected wherever she lives and works, and if she chooses not to wear the veil, the exact same should apply. They highlight that one of the inherent beauties of Islam is that there is choice, and that Muslims are specifically told in the Quran that there is no compulsion (*ikrah*) in the matters of religion—that Islam teaches that the sincerity of intentions and what's in the hearts of Muslims is what matters. Moreover, these Muslims insist that men, not Islam, have been responsible for the suppression of women's rights.

To that end, it appears that the jury is hung on whether the veil is obligatory (*wajib/fard*) or only recommended (*mustahab*) in Islam. But what is certain is that Muslim women are encouraged to dress modestly to safeguard their honor and dignity, and that the veil is not a tool of female oppression, but a sign of propriety and a means of protection against the menacing eyes of male strangers.

## POLYGAMY

Islam wasn't the first religion to permit polygamy, nor did Islam introduce it. To the contrary, Islam was the first faith to actually *limit* the number of wives according to strict conditions. In the pre-Islamic era, polygamy was practiced not only by the Arabs, but also by many other cultures around the world.

To this day, polygamy is widely practiced in parts of Africa. It is well known, for example, that President Jacob Zuma of South Africa has three wives and twenty children, not to mention the numerous "love children" that he's fathered. In addition, there are some fundamentalist sects of Mormonism that practice polygamy today in the state of Utah in the US.

The abolition of arcane or unjust customs that are practiced for centuries by suddenly issuing one sweeping ruling is both naïve and impractical. Islam took this into consideration and made a series of sensible laws by which it was able to enforce a gradual abolition of the previously common practice of marrying an unlimited number of wives.[7] In pre-Islamic Arabia, men could marry as many women as they wanted, but when Islam came, it limited the number of wives to up to four at one time: *"...Marry women of your choice, two, three, or four."*[8] There is, however, a most important condition which must be considered before marrying more than one wife. That is, treating *all* the wives equally, which is something that's basically impossible to achieve in today's society, due to the multitude of financial and social complexities.

The Prophet warned men against not treating wives equally by saying that a man who has two wives and does not treat them equally will suffer in this life.

The following Quranic verse confirms that treating one's wives equally is a difficult task, and that regardless of how conscientiously a man tries to do so, he won't be able to treat them all the same: *"You will never be able to be completely fair and just between women, no matter how hard you try."*[9] The tone of this verse can be interpreted as essentially telling Muslim men to forget about marrying more than one wife. The Prophet is the only man in Islam to be granted Quranic permission to have more than four wives, given his extraordinary personality and manners that enabled him to be truly just and equitable in all his marital affairs. (As explained in the previous chapter, Muhammad married most of his wives for humane and political reasons).

As such, and since the equal treatment of several wives is basically impossible, a man should marry only one wife: *"... But if you fear that you shall not be able to deal justly [with your wives], then only one wife."*[10] This religious law was enforced more than fourteen centuries ago, and it should be reiterated that Islam neither introduced nor enforced polygamy. That's because polygamy was a deeply entrenched practice that existed in Arabia well before the arrival of Islam. If anything, Islam dealt with the matter in a practical manner, without causing major upheaval in Arabian society at the time. This clearly highlights that in Islam monogamy is the rule and polygamy is the exception.

For example, Islam permitted exceptions in certain cases, such as during and after battles in which many men were killed, leaving widows and orphans without any means of financial support. Consequently, marriage to such women (as the Prophet himself did several times) was a virtue, because it provided them with an upright life and prevented women from going astray. In addition, if a woman had a chronic disease which made her unable to perform her marital obligations, or if she was infertile, the husband was permitted to marry another wife who would be entitled to exactly the same rights as the first wife. Accordingly, Islam permitted the exception of polygamy for the aforementioned specific reasons in order to reduce the probability of lust-only relationships and the ugly social consequences that result from them.

### INHERITANCE

In the pre-Islamic era, all women, rich and poor, were deprived of the right of inheritance. However, with the arrival of Islam, they were granted a definite share of the inherited estate, despite the opposition voiced by many Arabs at the time who considered that the right of inheritance was a benefit for men only. This was believed because men at the time were the ones who defended the tribe, fought its enemies, and were responsible for all of their family's expenses.

In most cases in Islam, the male heir inherits double the inheritance share of the female: *"God directs you as regards your children's inheritance: to the male a portion equal to that of two females."*[11] But a quick opinion here can easily lead to the sweeping generalization that Islam treats females unjustly for not granting them the same inheritance as males. However, Islam is not guilty of such an injustice, since the difference in the inheritance of males and females has nothing to do with favoring males. Rather, it is based upon the responsibilities which are obligatory for men and not for women. According to Islamic law, it is a man's duty to maintain and provide for his wife, children, and members of his family, which might include his father, mother, brothers, and sisters if they are not able to support themselves. His wife, on the other hand, is not charged with any financial responsibilities. She is not financially responsible for herself, however wealthy she may be, while her husband is fully responsible for her well-being. When carefully analyzing this specific situation, it becomes apparent that when she gets half of her husband's estate, her financial position could actually become superior to his.

There are also certain cases referred to in the Quran and explained in detail in Islamic law as to when the female's share of inheritance equals that of the male. Such a case is when the deceased person, man or woman, is childless and his or her parents are dead, and he or she leaves maternal brothers and/or sisters, each of whom receives an equal share of the inheritance. Furthermore, if a man's wife—who had a daughter by him or by a former husband—dies, her daughter inherits double what her father or stepfather inherits.

## TESTIMONY IN COURT

In general, Islamic law does not consider the testimony of one man equal to the testimony of two women in *all* matters, since there are some cases when the testimony of men is not accepted in matters that specifically concern women. This indicates that the testimony is not based upon the sex of the witness, but on his or her experience and knowledge.

At the time of the Prophet and in affairs that involved purchasing, selling, and other financial transactions, the experience of women was limited when compared to that of men, who spent most of their time looking after their trade. Accordingly, this rule applied in such cases since the experience of one man in financial dealings at the time was equal to the experience of two women. Thus, it was not a matter of lack of confidence in women or considering them inferior to men, but more a matter of experience and real practice in the broader dealings of business.

Today, a judge has the right to accept the testimony of one woman if he deems it fit to do so. Furthermore, no Muslim judge would accept the testimony of an illiterate, inexperienced man and refuse the testimony of an educated woman who is successful in her career. In other words, basic common sense is applied.

### CHAPTER 4, VERSE 34

In addition to the misunderstandings in the West about the four teachings of Islamic law presented earlier, one of the most debated verses in the Quran in relation to women is to be found in chapter 4:

> *Men are the protectors and supporters of women*
> *(qawwamuna ala al-nisaa),*
> *because God has given one more means than the other,*
> *and because they provide them with their property.*
> *So women of integrity are humble,*
> *guardians in absentia by God's protection.*
> *As for those of whom you fear perversity,*
> *admonish them [first];*
> *refuse to share their beds [second];*

*and [last] smack them [or turn away from them]*
*(idrubuhunna).*
*But if they obey you,*
*Then seek no means against them.*

The main topic of this chapter, titled "Women," is marital and social harmony, and the ethical duties, rules, and laws that should be obeyed to keep this harmony intact. When the thirty-fourth verse of chapter 4 is taken out of context, it can easily give the wrong impression—that women are commanded to obey their husbands under any circumstance—and when they don't, it's legitimate to use violence against them. Authentic Islamic tradition confirms that the Prophet never hit any of his wives and that he treated them all with utmost respect. So why would any Muslim man do what Muhammad didn't do?

The verse's "three-step approach" is often called a "reform" over the violent and patriarchal practices of seventh-century Arabia when the Quran was formulated. Women at the time of the primitive al-Jahiliyya period were also known to be promiscuous, with adultery and prostitution rampant throughout the quarters of Arabia. This meant that families were constantly threatened by the possibility of divorce and, thus, broken homes.

Because of the variability of the Arabic language, the above phrase *qawwamuna ala al-nisaa* can be understood as "watch over," "protect," "support," "attend to," "look after," or "be in charge of." In addition, the Arabic word *idrubuhunna* can be broadly interpreted as "smack them." Some Quranic scholars and translators (i.e., Majid Fakhry) do in fact interpret *idrubuhunna* as "smack them" or "beat them," while others (i.e., Ahmed Ali) indicate that it can equally mean "turn away from them," "go along with them," or "strike out on a journey," as in "*hit* the road" in colloquial English. As such, this much-disputed verse is open to several interpretations, depending on what one is trying to extract from the text. If one looks to the Quran to justify violence against women, then the former meaning can be extrapolated, but if one views the Quran as empowering women, then the latter meaning can be used. For the sake of argument—and if the former meaning was implied—the verse was not a license for battery, most Islamic scholars say, with other interpretations defining the heaviest instrument a man could have employed as a wooden twig commonly used as a toothbrush (or *sewaak*) to "smack them." At any rate, Sheikh Ali Gomaa, the Islamic scholar who currently serves as Egypt's grand *mufti*, has reiterated that some Quranic verses must be viewed *only* through the prism of their era. In this case, the era was al-Jahiliyya, which was characterized by brutal male practices that Islam was trying to gradually reform and bring out of darkness. It is important to note that up until the nineteenth century, European law allowed a man to beat his wife as much as he wanted as long as he did not endanger her life, and even allowed the use of whips and clubs,[12] so what Islam was trying to implement in the seventh century was quite revolutionary.

The whole idea behind the verse is not to punish one's wife. Rather, it's because of fear of sexual impropriety (considered a major sin in Islam) that the husband would take these phased steps to try to bring their relationship to where it's supposed to be. That is, it's only a gesture of displeasure. Lastly, it's clear that 4:34 cannot be understood without the general Quranic vision of an ideal relationship between spouses, as described in 30:21:

*And among the signs of God*
*is having created mates for you from yourselves*
*that you may feel at home with them,*
*creating love and compassion between you.*
*Surely there are signs in that*
*for people who reflect.*

## CONCLUSION

In Muslim communities, the concept of respect and the presence of a woman in public are, for better or for worse, intertwined. In most parts of south Asia and the Middle East, there are still relatively few opportunities for women to work outside the home, but the lack of education is mainly to blame. Only half of the women in the Arab world today are literate, and only 45 percent of south Asian women can read and write.[13] Female activists across the region have to work hard to defeat the primitive and un-Islamic idea that the only role fit for a woman is to raise a family, and that she should not leave the house unless she has permission from her father or husband. These are examples of arcane customs that need major reform to help women achieve their full potential in Muslim societies.

Women comprise only 15 percent of the membership in Asia's parliaments, and in Arab countries 8 percent of parliamentarians are female, according to the 2005 UN Arab Human Development Report. Based on such data, it is inaccurate to say that women in Muslim countries enjoy the freedom and respect that the Prophet had intended. On the other hand, it would also be incorrect to say that women in Islam have no rights today. They do, but not enough.

There are, nonetheless, numerous examples of Muslim women of power and influence, such as Benazir Bhutto, the late Prime Minister of Pakistan (1988-90 and 1993-96); Kaqusha Jashari, Chairperson of the Executive Council of the Republic of Kosovo (1987-89); and Tansu Ciller, the Turkish Premier (1993-96); among many others.

Women in Islam are supposed to be a symbol of love, family unity, and beauty that should be protected. They are also supposed to be the center of society, commanding both social prestige and respect. The Prophet Muhammad even said that, "Paradise lies under the feet of mothers."[14] However, there is a yawning gap between the ways women are being treated in Muslim countries today and how they *should* be treated by men, based on the Prophet's revolutionary teachings in the seventh century.

It is paramount to realize that the lack of freedom Muslim women suffer from today has nothing to do with the correct interpretation and application of the teachings of Muhammad; rather, it has to do with ignorance, poverty, and the inability to separate old tribal customs from true Islam. The hope is that Muslim societies push for an updated and more flexible interpretation of dated traditions, and openly discuss the numerous problems being caused by backward, male-dominated thinking, so that Muslim women can enjoy the full rights that the Prophet Muhammad had originally intended.

# MYTH FIVE:

### Islam Was Spread with the Sword

Made popular in Europe nearly one thousand years ago, the myth that Islam was spread with the sword is still thriving today. When some Westerners think about Muslims, they're typically pictured as wild-eyed religious fanatics with a sword or ticking bomb in one hand and a Quran in the other. This warped image has ossified in the minds of non-Muslims in our current era because of decades of incessant stereotyping by Hollywood and the Western media.

Whether it's because of the blanket stereotyping by Hollywood directors or because of superficial knowledge, Western culture often presumes that Islam is an aggressive, militaristic religion that rabidly imposed itself on its subjects at sword-point. This is a deeply inaccurate interpretation of the faith's period of expansion.

## The First Caliphs of Islam

When the Muslims ventured out of Arabia in 634, they were not driven by a raging urge to start a "holy war" against non-Muslims. There were, of course, battles fought during the expansion period of Islam, but battles are an inevitable part of the process of conquering nations. There was also a desire to spread the universal message of Muhammad. However, given the underlying principles and theologies of Islam, the main objective was *not* to instill fear into the conquered subjects. The unity of the Arab-Muslims would be preserved by an outwardly directed offensive which was first and foremost fuelled by trade and economic motives.[1]

When the Prophet Muhammad died in 632, almost all of Arabia was united through Islam. This in itself was a considerable accomplishment since the Bedouin tribes of Arabia had been plagued by disunity and endless internecine warfare. As Muhammad—who never intended for an overarching Islamic Caliphate to be established after his death—hadn't nominated a successor, conflicts emerged between his relatives, followed by tribal rebellions.

These conflicts came to an end when a deal was made between the closest companions of the Prophet. A successor of Muhammad and a temporal leader of the Islamic polity (a caliph) would take the leadership; thus, the Arab-Muslims started their expansionist campaigns. The tribes that fought one another became united once again, creating great concern for the two superpowers dominating the Middle East at the time: the Greek-Christian Byzantine Empire and Sassanid Zoroastrian Persia (present-day Iran).

The first caliph was Muhammad's closest companion and father-in-law Abou Bakr, but the Islamic conquests actually started during the reign of the second caliph, Omar. In 634, Omar conquered Damascus, and two years later his talented army chief, Khalid ibn al-Waleed, destroyed Emperor Heraclius's Byzantine military at the battle of Yarmouk, driving it away from Syria. The Arab-Muslims then invaded Mesopotamia (present-day Iraq), and by 642 they occupied Persia and Egypt. From Egypt, further campaigns conquered the whole of North Africa.

Meanwhile, the nascent Islamic Caliphate was temporarily impacted yet again by infighting among the Arab-Muslim tribes that began to form separate states. (There's an old saying in the Middle East that has withstood the test of time: "The only thing that Arabs have agreed upon is to disagree!") The third caliph, Othman, was murdered, and a fourth leader was chosen—Muhammad's cousin, Ali ibn abi Talib. The intertribal fighting continued and Ali was assassinated in Kufa (in current-day Iraq) in 661. His disciples refused to obey the successor, Muawiya of Damascus (from the Arabian Umayya tribe), and proclaimed autonomy. This was the definitive schism or fracture between the majority of Sunni Muslims and the Shia minority. Many other minor sects appeared later, but this rupture remains until today.

Ali's death ended the "classic" caliphate, comprised of the four closest companions to the Prophet: Abou Bakr, Omar, Othman, and Ali, known as the *Rashidun* (or the "rightly guided" caliphs). The classic caliphate lasted for twenty-nine years, and it's the only period that experienced a real

Islamic *umma*, or a quasi-utopian cross-border community of Muslims. It's hard to imagine that such an umma can ever be emulated, because the four caliphs were leaders of supreme virtue who possessed the spark of true enlightenment passed on directly to them by the Prophet. After the end of the classic caliphate, Muawiya started to rule more like a king from Damascus. Going forward, the seat of power was to be inherited by the ruler's son or a close relative, and rule was exerted with the help of a centralized social structure which wasn't typical of Muslim societies. Muawiya founded the first "dynasty" of rulers, the Umayyads, but their power materialized only after the new ruler, Abd el-Malik ibn Marawan, took power later in 685.

## THE UMAYYADS

Under the Umayyads (661 to 750), the overall Islamic Caliphate was ascending to its zenith because trade routes could be made undisturbed from Spain all the way to India and China. Unlike other conquerors, Arab-Muslims learned peacefully from other nations, adopting their ways of state ruling, army organization, and navigation. They also learned from the sciences and the arts of their subjects. Above all, Muslims were tolerant of non-Muslims, especially the "People of the Book" (the Jews and Christians).

The Arab-Muslims had learned a great deal from the Prophet's position toward converting to Islam. When he was in Medina, Muhammad would receive many tribal leaders from all over Arabia, especially Jews from Yemen, who were curious to learn about this new religion. They would spend several days in his hospitality, asking numerous questions about Islam. Many times, they would simply tell him that they didn't believe in his message and that they would never convert to Islam. Without showing any annoyance whatsoever, or enforcing any Islamic ideas upon them, the Prophet would generously ask them to stay longer in Medina if they wished before embarking on their trips back home. At the end of these meetings, the highly tolerant Muhammad would frequently quote the following verse: *"For you, your religion; for me, my religion."*[2]

## EXPANSION INTO SPAIN

The spread of Islamic principles continued and reached Spain in 711. Seven years later, the Arab and Moor Muslims crossed the Pyrenees Mountains, reaching central France, where they were stopped by the Franks at Tours in 732. Nevertheless, by this time, the originally Bedouin tribesmen of Arabia had carved out the largest Islamic region that the world had yet seen. Some scholars, such as military historian and Senior Fellow at the Hoover Institution Victor Davis Hanson, have suggested that Tours, which is poorly recorded in contemporary sources, was a construct of Western mythmaking, especially when it's viewed as a major turning point in world history. Hanson has also indicated (in his 2001 book titled *Carnage and Culture*) that a Muslim victory might have been preferable to the continued brutal Frankish dominance of Gaul (present-day France).

The Arab and Moor Muslims in Spain focused their attention on what was called *al-Andalus* in southern Spain (Andalusia), and built a culture far superior to anything the Spaniards had ever known. Reigning with justice, they improved trade and agriculture, introduced public sanitation systems, patronized the arts, and established Cordoba as the most sophisticated city in Europe. The land ownership system from the Roman times remained largely intact as Muslim leaders rarely dispossessed landowners, while the introduction of new crops and irrigation techniques led to a remarkable expansion of agriculture.

The Muslims ruled Spain prosperously for nearly eight hundred years (from 711 to 1492), and during that time the non-Muslim subjects flourished in tandem. Christian and Jewish minorities thrived in the Muslim communities of the Middle East for centuries. Countries such as Morocco, Egypt, Palestine, Jordan, Lebanon, and Syria all had (and still have) Christian and Jewish populations. The Islamic presence in Spain was a great example of the positive contribution of Islam to human civilization, as well as successful dialogue among the Abrahamic faiths.

If Islam preached that all people of other religions are supposed to be killed or forced to become Muslims, how did all of these non-Muslims survive for so long in the Islamic Caliphate? Moreover, if we consider the small number of Muslims who initially spread Islam from Spain and Morocco in the west and then eventually to India and China in the east, we would realize that they were far outnumbered to force the indigenous people to convert to a new religion against their will. As a result of this Islamic spirit of tolerance and respect of other religions, the Islamic Caliphate had significant staying power, and its citizens were proud to be part of it. Everywhere their armies spread, no forceful or obligatory conversions to the new faith followed, adhering to the Islamic principles of tolerance which are clearly laid out in the Quran.

## THE ABBASIDS

During the Umayyad Caliphate, many extremist subjects wrongfully felt that they didn't pay enough attention to proactively converting non-Muslims. Religious discontent emanating from Persia and Mesopotamia caused major riots in Damascus, resulting in a big rebellion in 750, the leader of which was Abou al-Abbas. After the Umayyads were overthrown by the Abbasids, they relocated to Spain, where they set up the Caliphate of Cordoba.

The Abbasid Caliphate (750 to 1258) established a new capital in Mesopotamia—Baghdad, which soon would have close to one million inhabitants. Special interest was placed on conversion to Islam and the adoption of the Arabic language as a way to learn and honor the Quran. Only Persia kept its language and its cultural identity, but it did eventually convert from Zoroastrianism to Islam.

### *JIZYA*

Muslims at that time weren't required to pay taxes, unlike the non-Muslims. Under the then-practiced Islamic law, *jizya* was a per-capita tax levied on a section of the state's non-Muslim citizens who met certain criteria. The tax was levied only on able-bodied adult males of military age and sufficient disposable income. There was no amount permanently fixed for the tax, though the payment usually depended on wealth. From the point of view of Muslim rulers, jizya was a material proof of the non-Muslims' acceptance of subjection to the Islamic state and its laws. In return, non-Muslim citizens (known as *dhimmis*) were permitted to practice their own faith, to be entitled to the Muslim state's protection from outside aggression, and to be exempted from military service.[3] Although Muslims weren't required to pay jizya, they were required to pay zaka (obligatory charity) amounting to 2.5 percent of their net annual income, which on average was higher than the jizya.

## THE DECLINE OF THE ISLAMIC CALIPHATE

The huge Islamic Caliphate was hard to control; its leaders were becoming complacent, and the Muslim trade routes were facing competition from rising powers. Over time, the political power of the Persians grew, and the Abbasids turned into mere puppets of the Persian rulers. Matters got even more complicated when the Muslim Seljuk-Turks, originally nomadic Mongolian tribes from Central Asia, occupied most of the Islamic near east, ruling it in the name of the Abbasids between 1055 and 1157, and their leader being a sultan. The Turks were highly skilled warriors, forcing the Byzantines to ask for help from Christian Europe. In my view, this is why the bloody Crusades originally started.

By the thirteenth century, the Islamic Caliphate was divided into small sultanates, and in 1258 the caliphate was officially over when the Mongols sacked Baghdad. When the Mongols invaded and conquered large portions of the Muslim regions, instead of eradicating the religion, they actually adopted it, a unique occurrence in history wherein the conquerors adopt the religion of the conquered. Since they were the victors, they could not have been forced to become Muslims. (The largest Muslim country in the world today is Indonesia, with 203 million followers of Islam, and it's important to emphasize that there were never any battles fought there).

After the demise of the Islamic Caliphate in 1258 and the fading of the Mongols, four imperial dominions were established between the thirteenth and early eighteenth centuries: the Afsharid and Safavid Dynasties in Iran, the Mughal Empire in India, and the Ottoman Empire in Anatolia, Syria, North Africa, and Arabia. These new empires, especially the Ottomans, all seemed to turn their backs on the egalitarian traditions of Islam and set up murderously sectarian regimes.

## THE OTTOMAN EMPIRE

The Ottoman Empire continued to rule in many of the Muslim countries. However, it's necessary to distinguish between the Islamic Caliphate and the Ottoman Empire. The Ottoman Empire was completely different in that it was structured around a brutal and oppressive political agenda, coupled with a relentless pursuit of power, which lasted from 1299 to 1924.

The Ottomans committed numerous atrocities which fanned the flames of hatred between Christians and Muslims, such as the alleged Armenian Genocide. The Armenian Genocide was the deliberate and systematic destruction of the Armenian population of the Ottoman Empire during and after World War I.[4] It was characterized by massacres and deportations involving forced marches under cruel conditions, with the total number of Armenian deaths estimated at approximately 800,000.[5] Other ethnic groups were similarly attacked by the Ottomans during this period, including the Assyrians and Greeks.

No such hubristic events occurred under the rule of the Islamic Caliphate. Rather, the spread of Islam was a positive phase in human history that led to remarkable contributions to Western civilization.

### ISLAM'S CONTRIBUTIONS TO WESTERN CIVILIZATION[6]

A summary of Islam's vast contributions to Western civilization is provided to highlight that the Muslims were not focused on looting and destruction when Islam was expanding. To the contrary, they were primarily driven by trade and commerce—the urge to improve their knowledge and to share it with others.

The period of the Abbasid dynasty witnessed the peak of the Islamic Caliphate—the Golden Age of Islam. One of its leaders, Abou Jaafar al-Mansur, helped establish the Palace of Wisdom in Baghdad in 762, a majestic library where the intelligentsia studied ancient philosophy and medicine, and learned the mathematics of India. The numbers that we use today were invented by mathematicians in India, but are known as "Arabic" numbers because the Arab-Muslims introduced them to Europe. Many classic works of antiquity that would otherwise have been forgotten were translated into Arabic and later into Turkish, Persian, and Hebrew, and when scholars began to translate Arabic works into Latin some three hundred years later, Europe was completely transformed. During this period, the Muslim world was also a melting pot of cultures, which collected and significantly advanced the knowledge gained from the ancient Roman, Greek, Hindu, and Chinese civilizations.

Literature and art also flourished throughout the Islamic Caliphate, while architecture grew vigorously with the construction of grand mosques and magnificent palaces. Al-Azhar, the world's second oldest surviving, degree-granting university (after the University of al-Qarawiyyin in Morocco), was founded in Cairo in 969. Arabesques reproduced plant and animal motifs, combining them with elegant lines of Arabic writings known as calligraphy. The collection of Asian-Muslim stories called "The Book of One Thousand and One Nights," narrated by the legendary Persian queen Scheherazade, has become a classic. In addition, Islamic science and culture pushed its contemporary Europe a few centuries forward. The Western world took many of the Muslim sources of science, philosophy, mathematics, and medicine—even the method of paper-making originally invented by the Chinese had reached Europe through the Muslims.

Algebra is an Arabic word, and it was the Muslim mathematician al-Khawarizmi (d. 840) that developed the subject from its Babylonian roots. Abou Bakr Razi (d. 925), known in the West as Rhazes, was the most influential of the Muslim alchemists who discovered and classified a large number of natural substances in experiments using sophisticated apparatus. The Muslim-Persian Ibn Seena (d. 1037), widely known as Avicenna, was a brilliant philosopher and medic who was famous even in Europe at the time. Abou Ali al-Haytham (d. 1039), or Alhazen, is known as the father of the science of optics, and, emerging from a thriving Islamic culture of curiosity and experiment, he was also one of the earliest experimental scientists who introduced the scientific method. Another major contributor to Western civilization was Ibn Rushd, known in European literature as Averroes (d. 1198).

Averroes, an Andalusian-Muslim, was a master of Islamic philosophy. He has also been described as the founder of secular thought and one of the spiritual fathers of Europe.[7]

Jalal al-Din Rumi (d. 1273), known to the English-speaking world simply as Rumi, was a Persian-Muslim poet. His poems have been widely translated into many languages and transposed into various formats. A Sufi (a Muslim who seeks the mystical dimension of Islam), Rumi was described as the most popular poet in the United States in 2007.[8] He sought ecstasy in poetry, dancing, singing, and music, and the members of the order that he founded in Konya are called the Whirling Dervishes, because of their spinning dance, which induces a mystical state of transcendence. An example of his poetry includes

"Not Christian or Jew or Muslim, not Hindu
Buddhist, Sufi, or Zen. Not any religion
or cultural system. I am not from the east
or the west, not out of the ocean or up
from the ground, not natural or ethereal, not
composed of elements at all. I do not exist,
am not an entity in this world or in the next,
did not descend from Adam and Eve or any
origin story. My place is placeless, a trace
of the traceless. Neither body or soul.
I belong to the beloved, have seen the two
worlds as one, and to the one call to know,
first, last, outer, inner, only that
breath, a breathing human being."[9]

The astrolabe, an ancient astronomical "computer" for solving problems relating to time and the position of the sun and stars in the sky, was perfected during the Islamic Caliphate, and was introduced to Europe from Islamic Spain in the early twelfth century. It was the most popular astronomical instrument until about 1650, when it was replaced by more specialized instruments.

Much of this learning and progress that was based on an intricate web of international trade can be linked to the origins of the Bedouin tribes of Arabia. Even prior to Islam, Mecca served as a center of trade and commerce. The tradition of the pilgrimage to Mecca became a center for exchanging ideas and goods, and as a result Islamic civilization grew and expanded on the basis of its merchant roots.

## THE MUSLIM TRADE ROUTES

As indicated earlier, Islam spread throughout the east, reaching maritime southeast Asia, with the Muslim merchants playing a crucial part in the spreading of their religion. Islam, along with its Sufi mystics, arrived in Hindu India via trade routes, subsequently becoming a major religion in the Indian subcontinent. Since the eighth century, Muslim traders had arrived in the coastal regions of western and southern India, including Surat in western Gujarat and the Malabar Coast in Kerala, and settled there. India, therefore, became a central part of the Muslim trade routes.[10]

By the tenth century, the Muslim trade routes connected Asia with the Mediterranean world. As they traveled, traders spread Islamic culture to Europe via the Levant, Sicily, and Spain. In Asia, they penetrated as far as China and journeyed over the ancient Silk Road. Muslim traders also traveled across northern Africa and as far as Timbuktu (present-day Mali) in the western part of the continent.

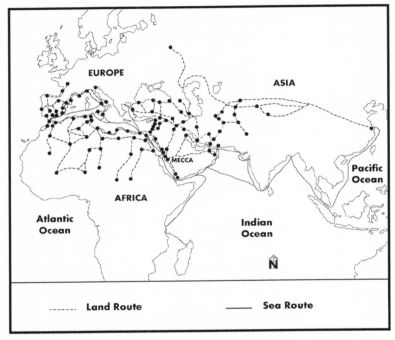

*Map 1. The Muslim Trade Routes*

## CONCLUSION

Islam teaches that a person's faith must be certain and sincere, so it's not something that can be forced upon others at sword-point. The British historian De Lacy Evans O'Leary wrote, "History makes it clear that the legend of fanatical Muslims sweeping through the world and forcing Islam at the point of the sword upon conquered races is one of the most fantastically absurd myths that historians have ever accepted."[11] Mark Glenn, the American-Catholic activist, confirms that non-Muslims were not converted by the sword as is commonly taught and believed in the West. Based on his research, Glenn confirms that Christians and Jews were allowed to keep and practice their religion during the reign of the Islamic Caliphate between 634 and 1258.[12]

In her book, *Allah is Completely Different*, the German orientalist Sigrid Hunke refuted the accusations that Islam was spread by the sword. She wrote,

The tolerance of the Arabs played an important role in the spreading of Islam, contrary to what has been falsely claimed, that it was spread by fire and the sword, which is an unjust and unverified accusation against Islam. Christians and Jews embraced Islam of their own free will. It is a well-known fact that Muslim armies never invaded south Asia or west Africa, yet Islam spread and flourished in these countries after Muslim merchants travelled with their merchandise to these countries. Muslim Sufis, with their peaceful attitude, also impressed the inhabitants of these lands. The natives of these distant countries saw for themselves the conduct, morals, and dealings of the Muslims, and accordingly, embraced Islam of their own free will.[13]

The Islamic Caliphate led to an unprecedented teaching of tolerance, acceptance, and respect of other religions, in addition to the transfer of wealth and knowledge via trade and commerce that vastly benefitted Western civilization. The benefits ranged from the advancement of medicine, optometry, and algebra, to the arts, literature, and poetry. If Islam was spread with the sword as alleged by many Western observers, then how come such large countries as Indonesia,

India, and Nigeria have so many Muslims today, when no wars of religious conversion were fought there? Why is Islam one of the fastest growing religions in the world today when it's actually the Judeo-Christian nations that are bombing and invading Muslim-majority states such as Afghanistan, Iraq, and Palestine? These historical and current events need to be put into perspective so that Western observers can come to terms with the actuality that Islam is not an inherently hostile and intolerant faith.

# MYTH SIX:

## Islam is an Inherently Hostile
## and Intolerant Faith

*God invites you into the abode of peace...*
*help each other to kindness and conscience,*
*and do not help each other*
*to conflict and animosity.*[1]

The vestiges of September 11, 2001, anxieties about Muslims, combined with silent racism, have reignited the myth that Islam is a religion driven by a violent and intolerant ideology that seeks to conquer any contradictory culture or faith. As a result, the myth of the fanatical intolerance of Islam has become one of the major distorted ideas in the West today.

Islam is not a violent religion. Some think that because a faction of extremist terrorists acts in the name of Islam, it is therefore an inherently violent faith. Islam is a peaceful religion, and the Quran teaches that all human life is sacred. In fact, the word "Islam" is derived from *salaam*, which means "peace" and "submission" in Arabic.

### THE PROPHET'S APPROACH TO CONFLICT

Although the Prophet Muhammad was born in the dark era of Arab belligerence, tribal hatred, and ignorance (al-Jahiliyya), he was a peace-loving man. Islam considers an attack on one single person an attack on all humankind: *"If anyone killed a person...it would be as if he killed all the people."* [2] In addition, the Quran doesn't consecrate warfare, clearly saying, *"There is no compulsion in religion."* [3]

To help the people of Mecca out of their sufferings, the Prophet took to preaching Islam among them in a peaceful way. Most of the people of Mecca were polytheists, so they refused to accept his teachings. They not only insulted and harmed him, but they used brute force to torture those people who had responded favorably to his teachings and become Muslims. Even in the face of their fierce opposition, the Prophet would give his polytheist enemies food. Yet this extraordinary gesture failed to soften them, and they continued to oppose Muhammad with all the forcefulness at their disposal. The Prophet always remained patient and didn't react to the polytheists' insults and tortures. Taking advantage of his peaceful nature, some polytheists went to his house to kill him while he was asleep. However, the Angel Gabriel warned him of the impending danger, and he managed to escape to Medina with his closest companion, Abou Bakr. Even with this attempt by his enemies, he bore no grudges against them. There were many other times that the polytheists of Mecca had tried to kill the Prophet, but he would miraculously escape every time. In fact, Muhammad's entire life was a defiance of extraordinary odds, giving us a hint that he was protected by a force that is beyond the visible world—a force that willed to see his message communicated to all humanity.

It's paramount to know that after the Prophet received his first revelations, he remained in Mecca for nearly twelve years without any aggression or retaliation whatsoever against its tribes, despite their nonstop torture of newly converted Muslims. Given what seemed to be a never-ending period of suffering for him, his family, and his followers, there were times when Muhammad questioned God about the length of this humiliation without any self-defense. It wasn't until he received the following verses (after he had moved to Medina) that the Prophet assumed the role of military strategist that was imposed upon him. After the revelation of these verses, which demonstrate the specific methods of dealing with aggressors, Muhammad was ordered by God to defend himself and his followers until the attackers backed down, paid the protective jizya (tax), or embraced Islam:

> *There is immunity from God*
> *and the Messenger of God*
> *for those polytheists*
> *with whom you have made treaties:*
> *So travel the earth for four months,*

*and know that you cannot thwart God,*
*and that it is God who thwarts the atheists.*
*A call from God and God's Messenger*
*to the people on the great day of pilgrimage:*
*that God and the Messenger of God*
*have nothing to do*
*with the polytheists.*
*So if you repent,*
*that is better for you;*
*but if you turn away,*
*know that you cannot thwart God.*
*And announce a painful penalty*
*for those who disbelieve.*
*Except those polytheists*
*with whom you have made a treaty*
*and they have not failed you in anything*
*and have not helped anyone against you;*
*fulfill your treaties with them*
*to the end of their term,*
*for God loves the conscientious.*
But when the sacred months are past,
then kill idolaters wherever you find them,
and capture them, and blockade them,
and watch for them at every lookout.
But if they repent and practice prayer
and give alms,
let them go their way;
for God is most forgiving and merciful.
*And if one of the polytheists*
*asks you for protection, then protect him,*

*until he hears the word of God:*
*then deliver him to a place safe for him.*
*That is because they are people*
*who do not know.*[4]

The verse that isn't italicized above is the so-called "Verse of the Sword," which, when quoted out of context and on a standalone basis, can be easily misinterpreted. As mentioned previously, the Quran has to be read within the context of *when* and *why* each of its verses was revealed. In this specific case, the Muslims had been suffering immensely for more than a decade and had been forced to leave their hometown of Mecca, reaching a breaking point. In God's view, the time for their justified self-defense had finally arrived.

The reader is reminded that there are violent statements in the Bible as well, which probably cause many Jews and Christians to grimace. There is the Book of Deuteronomy 7:16 of the Old Testament (New International Version): "You must destroy all the peoples the Lord your God gives over to you." There is also Psalm 137:9 (New Living Translation): "Happy is the one who takes your babies and smashes them against the rocks!" Another promises, "Morning by morning will I put to death all the sinners in the land, so that all evildoers may be cut off from Jerusalem," (Psalm 101:8, Bible in Basic English). After David performs heroically in battle, the Israelite women, "...danced and sang: 'Saul has slain his thousands, and David his tens of thousands,'" (I Samuel 18:7, New International Version). In addition, the Book of Joshua is full of bloody battles waged at the command of God. Do these passages mean that the Bible is a book of violence and hatred, and that modern Jews and Christians must read the stories and celebrations of the Jews as a guide for their behavior in the present? Of course not, because these passages pertained to a particular time and set of circumstances. The exact same approach should be applied to the so-called "Verse of the Sword" in the Quran. Furthermore, and according to the vast majority of Muslim scholars, the fact that a few religiously ignorant Muslim extremists interpret specific verses in the Quran as being supportive of their terrorist acts is a gross error.

The Prophet Muhammad wasn't hostile or aggressive in dealing with his opponents. He was distinguishing between covenanters, warriors, and non-Muslims. He didn't violate treaties or act treacherously toward his enemies—to the contrary, he dealt with each of them according to basic peace and wartime parameters. Ibn al-Qayyem al-Jawziyya, the Muslim philosopher who lived in Damascus in the 1300s, summarized the fighting manners of the Prophet in his book *Zaad al-meaad*:

After God had ordered Muslims to fight the disbelievers, the Prophet had classified them into three categories: covenanters, warriors, and non-Muslims. He instructed the honoring of treaties which were entered with the covenanters as long as they honored their promises, but if he feared that they would violate the treaties, he would terminate the written agreements and would not fight them except after notifying them duly about the termination of the treaty.[5]

Peace was exchanged under certain conditions, and war was preceded with objective premises aimed at attaining the peace, such as the propagation for embracing Islam by free will or paying the protective jizya. Otherwise, if they insisted on aggression and fought the Islamic propagation, the Muslims would be forced to fight them back.

Although war is a ruthless process, the Prophet had legislated basic morals and principles governing the manners of the Muslim fighter, while imposing severe punishments on the violators. In Islam, war must not be used except under specific permissible means and fair methods, and Muslims are forbidden to initiate hostilities. The Quran permits only defensive warfare and condemns war as being a daunting evil. Aggression is strictly prohibited, and there must be no preemptive strikes. In sum, the essential rules that organized Muhammad's relations with his enemies culminated in the following:[6]

1. Fighting only if attacked first by the enemy
2. Focusing only on the actual (tactical) objectives of war
3. Avoiding anything related to hatred, treachery, revenge, or egotistical retaliation
4. Preservation of the natural environment
5. Not confronting non-warriors such as women, children, and old people
6. Religious forgiveness—not killing priests or rabbis unless *they* initiate the fighting against Muslims or support the enemies who are fighting the Muslims
7. Respecting the sacred places of others and avoiding their churches and synagogues
8. Ceasing hostilities and beginning negotiations the moment the enemy asks for peace.

Moreover, when Muhammad marched on Mecca in 631 with a force said to number more than ten thousand men, there were minimal casualties. When he took control of the town, he declared an extraordinary amnesty for all past offences and pardoned his opponents. As a result, most Meccans converted peacefully to Islam. Is this the behavior of a warmonger who wantonly applied the "Verse of the Sword" against the unbelievers?

Therefore, those who accuse the Prophet of being a ruthless warlord are unaware of these exceptionally humane manners and morals that he had established for his soldiers. It is, of course, painful to see how far removed the radical Muslims of our era have become from the Prophet's teachings, but it is vital to realize that Muslim extremists comprise a small percentage of the followers of Islam worldwide. Those with hateful ideologies—who commit terrorist atrocities—have a warped state of mind and are the *real* enemies of Islam, because they have criminalized and stigmatized the whole Muslim community in the West.

### ISLAMOPHOBIA

So-called "radical Islam" is not a religion. It's an extreme political ideology that abuses monotheism to justify mass murder, oppression, and intolerance. The bizarre objective of radicals is world domination and an end to all religions, except its own deeply perverted version of Islam. The followers of radical Islam want to kill those standing in its way, including non-radical Muslims, Jews, Christians, and Hindus, thus contributing to global Islamophobia.

Islamophobia is the irrational fear of Islam or Muslims predicated on the belief that all the followers of Islam hate non-Muslims.[7] Islamophobia is also a global fear that stems from centuries of prejudice and an intractable lack of understanding. The current Islamophobia—which in some instances has been fueled by real grievances where unjust policies have stimulated anti-Western feelings (i.e., the invasion of Iraq in 2003), and where knee-jerk terrorist acts have, in turn, ignited a global fear of all Muslims—is a vicious cycle that must be broken.

Islamophobia is caused by the incorrect application of Islam by Muslim extremists, in addition to a significant lack of knowledge in the West about this magnificent yet much misunderstood faith. Islamophobia also contends that Islam doesn't separate the secular from the spiritual, and that religion shouldn't be separated from the state. To get rid of this lingering phobia, more Muslim clerics need to accept that Islam is intended to be a dynamic faith which has to be in sync with its times, because it is always dangerous to isolate religious ideas from contemporary thought. Furthermore, Muslim leaders should promote that the separation of religion and state is essential for the religion's success as a peaceful and tolerant way of life.

There are numerous examples over the last forty years of how a few radical Islamists have set a disgraceful example of their people for the world, causing them to be stereotyped. It also doesn't help the already tarnished image of Islam when a tiny percentage of Arab-Muslims cheer at extremist-masterminded atrocities such as 9/11, the train bombings in Madrid on March 11, 2004, and the July 7,

2005, explosions in London, which in aggregate killed 3,740 innocent people, including Muslims. The horrific events of 9/11 were, without doubt, one of the lowest points in human history, because of the deaths of so many innocent civilians, and because a divine faith was so misinterpreted and violated to meet the sick and twisted political objectives of mass murderers.

Terrorism cannot be justified under any valid interpretation of Islam. The Quran, taken in its entirety, gives a message of hope, faith, tolerance, respect of other beliefs, and peace. The overwhelming message is that peace is to be found through faith in God and justice among fellow human beings. Most moderate Muslim leaders and scholars speak out against terrorism in all its forms, and offer explanations of misinterpreted verses and teachings, although this constructive stance is often ignored by the Western media.

Because Islam has a major image problem in the West, its leaders and scholars are starting to be much more unified on this foremost issue. They are condemning those so-called Muslims who have fallen over the edge into terrorist networks, trying to pound into their heads that there is absolutely no justification or glorification whatsoever in Islam that's associated with killing innocent civilians. Some of the more articulate and moderate scholars in Islam today include Sheikh Hamza Yusuf of the Zaytuna College in Berkeley, California, and Amr Khaled in Egypt. In 2007, Amr Khaled was voted by *Time* magazine as one of the "100 most influential people in the world." Although by no means a household name in the West, for a segment of the Islamic world the youthful Egyptian scholar is a "rock star."

## Terrorism and *Jihad*

So-called "Islamic terrorism" is an oxymoron, because Islam strongly condemns violence and terrorist acts. At any rate, the term "Islamic terrorism" first entered the lexicon of the Western media on a Beirut morning in 1983, when two suicide bombers destroyed the barracks of American and French peacekeepers. The American toll came to 241 dead; the planners were radical Shiites inspired by the Iranian leader Ayatollah Khomeini, who claimed credit in the name of a so-called Islamic "holy war."

One of the biggest misunderstandings and confusions related to Islam is that all Muslims promote violence to spread their religion by the sword and to kill all unbelievers in some kind of holy war. The truth is that Islam doesn't acknowledge the widely misused term "holy war." Islam regards wars as being either unjust or just. According to the Iranian-American scholar Reza Aslan, the term "holy war" originated not from Islam but from the Christian Crusaders who first used it to give theological legitimacy to what was in reality a battle for land and trade routes.

The word *jihad* is derived from the Arabic word *juhd* which means "to strive" and "to exert one's utmost efforts." These efforts are divided into two forms: the "greater jihad" and the "lesser jihad," summarized as follows.[8]

| GREATER JIHAD | LESSER JIHAD |
|---|---|
| ◆ Effort made by oneself, where one endeavors to repel all evil and temptations.<br>◆ To purify one's soul from vice, especially the dark vices of jealousy, envy, and hatred.<br>◆ Constant self-improvement through hard and honest work, education, or athletics.<br>◆ Prudent and constructive spending of one's wealth.<br>◆ Taking care of, and protecting, one's family when under siege.<br>◆ Striving to be brought into the grace of God. | ◆ Effort made in fighting a just and righteous war.<br>◆ Military effort is included as an option, but only as a last resort of self-defense, and certainly not to "spread Islam by the sword." |

A righteous and just war according to the laws of Islam is to repel the enemy's attack. The following Quranic verses permit Muslims to fight only the enemy who attacks them: "*Victims of aggression are given license because they have been done injustice*"[9] as well as

> *...if anyone is aggressive toward you,*
> *then you be aggressive toward him,*
> *with the equivalent of the aggression toward you.*

> *But be conscious of God,*
> *and know that God is with the conscientious.*[10]

These verses prove that despite the permission to fight in self-defense, Muslims are warned not to go beyond defending themselves to the extent of transgression.

If Muslims learn that their enemy wants peace and is willing to cease all forms of aggression, Islam commands its followers to agree to their enemy's request: *"But if the enemy inclines toward peace, then you also incline toward peace, and place your trust in God."*[11] Furthermore, Islam calls for peaceful co-existence with others and the establishment of goodwill with them, provided that they don't attack Muslims:

> *God has not forbidden you*
> *to be charitable and just*
> *to those who have not*
> *fought you over religion*
> *or driven you from your homes,*
> *for God loves the just.*[12]

The aim of Islam is to spread and establish peace and tolerance among people, and to urge them to cooperate with each other for the welfare of humanity. To that end, the allegations found in the majority of the Western media today that Islam is a religion that preaches violence and terrorism are unjustified accusations with no foundation in the Muslim faith.

## SUICIDE BOMBERS

An offshoot of terrorism is the trend of endless suicide bombings in Israel, Afghanistan, Pakistan, and elsewhere—senseless acts of despair and self-destruction that have no basis whatsoever in Islam. Suicide bombers are so desperate that they don't comprehend the full implications of their atrocious actions. They most likely suffer from a variety of psychological disorders, such as severe anxiety and depression, impacting their judgment. Add the fact that the suicide bombers are brainwashed and are given lots of cash by radical religious clerics, and the lethal combination of terrorism and made-up Islam is ignited.

The Taliban, for example, advertises that they actively train children from Pakistan, Afghanistan, Central Asia, and the Middle East to be suicide bombers. To solve this tragedy, there needs to be a fight against poverty and a commitment to providing education and opportunity so that children aren't turned into murderers, thinking that suicide and death are their only escape from a hopeless life. According to Zahid Hussain, the Pakistan correspondent for *The Times* of London, almost 90 percent of suicide bombers in Pakistan are twelve to eighteen years old.

Several authenticated hadith are clear about what happens to anyone who commits suicide: "A man was inflicted with wounds and he committed suicide, and so God conveyed: 'My slave has caused death on himself hurriedly, so I'll forbid paradise for him.'"[13] In addition, "And if somebody commits suicide with any method in this world, he'll be continuously tortured in that same way on the day of judgment."[14]

Many more hadith condemn suicide, but I'd like to make reference to the Quran as well. Among the verses against suicide, here is one that makes it clear that the taking of one's life is strongly prohibited and that there's no reward for anyone who commits it:

> *And do not kill yourselves;*
> *for God has been merciful to you.*
> *And if any do that,*
> *with hostility and injustice,*
> *then We will cause them great suffering.*[15]

In the Western media, we also often hear about the so-called reward of seventy-two virgins in paradise for suicide bombers. But are there any Islamic teachings we can point to endorsing that? The answer is no. The seventy-two virgins are not mentioned anywhere in the Quran. Moreover, there are no authentic hadith by the Prophet that support this most bizarre allegation.

## TERRORISM: A GLOBAL CRISIS

For centuries, false stories have been fabricated about Muslims and their alleged violence against Jews and Christians. Contrary to the depictions created by their enemies, the vast majority of Muslims have been kind to them, treating them with great respect, as Islam was founded on many of the religious precepts of the Jews and Christians.

Islam does not have a monopoly on murderous zealotry, an occurrence that has produced equally shameful displays in both Judaism and Christianity. In the Western media, much too often one senses the tendency to conclude that *only* Muslims and *all* Muslims are potential terrorists, or that Islam is inherently linked to violence, despite the occurrence of non-Muslim religion-inspired bloodshed. Such events include the Catholic Irish Republican Army's (IRA) bombings in Northern Ireland and England, where approximately 1,800 people were killed between 1969 and the early 1990s;[16] the events of Jonestown (the informal name for the "Peoples Temple," an American cult led by Jim Jones), where 919 people committed suicide in Guyana in 1978;[17] and the burning of the Branch Davidian compound of born-again Christian David Koresh outside of Waco, Texas, in 1993, where Koresh, fifty-eight other adults, and twenty-one children were killed[18]—all examples where religious beliefs went terribly wrong.

More recently, the international community was shocked when President George W. Bush used the term "crusade" to describe the 2003 invasion of Iraq,[19] a war that was based on false allegations against Iraq that it had weapons of mass destruction and which has caused the death of an estimated one hundred thousand innocent Iraqi civilians.[20] In addition, Bush once told Texas evangelist James Robinson, "I feel like God wants me to run for president. I can't explain it, but I sense my country is going to need me. Something is going to happen...I know it won't be easy on me or my family, but God wants me to do it."[21] Lieutenant General William G. Boykin, who was the US Deputy Undersecretary of Defense for Intelligence during the George W. Bush administration, is known to have said, "The war on terror was a fight against Satan," and bragged that he once told a Somali-Muslim, "My

God was bigger than his. I knew that my God was a real God and his was an idol."[22]

The Jewish Defense League (JDL) which was founded in 1969 by extremist Rabbi Meir Kahane in New York City was created for the sole purpose of protecting Jews. Federal Bureau of Investigation statistics show that from 1980 to 1985, fifteen terrorist attacks were attempted in the US by members of the JDL, which has been described as "a proscribed terrorist group."[23]

Baruch Goldstein, an American-born Israeli physician who committed the Cave of the Patriarchs massacre in the city of Hebron in 1994, killed twenty-nine innocent Muslims at prayer in a mosque and seriously wounded another 125 in a shooting rampage.[24] The Israeli attack on Gaza in the winter of 2008–2009 resulted in the killing of 1,166 Palestinians (and only thirteen Israelis).[25] More than four hundred thousand Gazans were left without running water, while four thousand homes were destroyed or badly damaged, leaving tens of thousands of people homeless; eighty government buildings were also hit.[26] During the attacks, the chief army rabbi, Brigadier General Avichai Rontzki, joined the Israeli troops in the field on a number of occasions, as did rabbis under his command. Officers and soldiers reported that they felt "spiritually elevated" and "morally empowered" by conversations with rabbis who gave them encouragement before the war with the Palestinians.[27] Do these atrocities indicate that *all* Israelis and Jews are violent? Absolutely not!

Lastly, during the Bosnian Genocide (which refers to either the atrocities committed by the Christian Serb and Croat forces in Srebrenica in 1995, or to the ethnic cleansing that took place during the 1992–1995 Bosnian War), an estimated twenty-six thousand Muslim civilians were systematically murdered.[28]

There are numerous examples of contemporary Christian and Jewish religion-inspired bloodshed and extremism, but the purpose of this book is *not* to point fingers at anyone. Rather, the purpose of mentioning these events is to simply show that Christians and Jews also suffer from the cancer of extremism and terrorism. Everywhere, people have appealed to religion to justify actions that most persons of goodwill condemn as contrary to their faith. Simply because people claim to belong to a particular religion does not mean that they fairly represent that tradition.[29] It merely means that groups of deceitful people can sometimes twist and manipulate religion for evil purposes.[30]

### Conclusion

Islam is a tolerant faith that calls upon all people to become united and to live together in friendship, despite the inherent differences between them:

> *O humankind, We created you*
> *from a male and a female,*
> *and We made you races and tribes*
> *for you to get to know each other.*[31]

As such, accusing the underlying principles of Islam of intolerance and violence is unfounded. If some individual Muslims are fanatics or terrorists, that doesn't mean that Islam as a whole should be held responsible for their actions.

It's essential to differentiate between the tolerant teachings and just principles of Islam and the appallingly irresponsible behavior of a few ignorant men and women who claim to be Muslims. We also must keep in mind that fanaticism isn't limited to the followers of a single religion, and that terrorism is a chronic global crisis.

# MYTH SEVEN:

## Judaism Is the Enemy of Islam

Moses is a highly venerated prophet in Islam. Muslims revere Moses (*Moussa* in Arabic) because God spoke to him directly, he relayed the Ten Commandments to humanity, and because he is mentioned 136 times in the Quran. The holy book of Islam also makes forty-three specific references to *Bani Israeel*, or the Children of Israel.

Throughout the Quran, Muslims are reminded that they're not the only ones who received guidance from God:

> *We revealed the Torah,*
> *in it guidance and light;*
> *the prophets who surrendered to God*
> *judge the Jews thereby,*

> *as do the rabbis and the learned,*
> *by what was entrusted to them*
> *in the Book of God...*
> *And We caused Jesus the Son of Mary*
> *to follow in their tracks, verifying*
> *what was there before him in the Torah;*
> *and We gave him the Gospel,*
> *with guidance and truth in it,*
> *also verifying what was there*
> *before him in the Torah.*[1]

In addition, the Quran commands Muslims to protect from harm not only mosques, but also synagogues and churches because God is worshipped therein. In 45:16, the holy book of Islam gives high praise to the followers of Moses when it says:

> *We did give the Children of Israel scripture,*
> *and wisdom, and prophethood;*
> *and We provided them with good things,*
> *and blessed them above all peoples of their time.*

So the question one needs to ask is this: how can it be said that Judaism is the enemy of Islam?

## The Similarities between Islam and Judaism

There seems to be a myth that Jews can't respect Islam or that Muslims can't respect Judaism. This is absurd because Judaism and Islam are, in fact, closer than any other two religions. Because Judaism and Islam share a common origin in the Middle East through Abraham and his descendants, both are considered Abrahamic religions. Islam and Judaism share the idea of a revealed scripture, and even though they differ over the precise text and its interpretations, the Torah and the Quran share common narrative as well as rulings. From this, they share many other fundamental religious concepts, such as the belief in a day of judgment.

Muslims commonly refer to the Jews (and Christians) as fellow "People of the Book": those who follow the same general teachings in relation to the worship of the one and only God worshipped by Abraham, and the toleration of people with different beliefs and faiths.

The main common practice between Judaism and Islam is the statement of the absolute unity of God. Islam and Judaism both consider the Christian doctrine of the Trinity and the belief of Jesus being God (in a literal sense) as against the tenets of monotheism. Idolatry, worshiping graven images, is likewise forbidden in both religions. The two faiths also share the central practices of fasting and almsgiving, as well as specific dietary laws. Under strict dietary teachings, permitted food is called kosher in Judaism and *halal* in Islam. Both religions prohibit the consumption of pork and forbid sexual relations outside of marriage. Both faiths also encourage modest attire for women and practice circumcision for newborn males.

The following table summarizes the primary beliefs and doctrines that are similar in both divine religions:

| BELIEFS AND DOCTRINES | JUDAISM | ISLAM |
|---|---|---|
| Type of Theism | Strict monotheism | Strict monotheism |
| Creation | One Creator-God | One Creator-God |
| Other Intangible Beings | Angels and demons | Angels (*malayka*) and demons (*jinn*) |
| Divinity of Jesus | Denied | Denied |
| Resurrection of Jesus | Denied | Denied |
| Mode of Divine Revelation | Through prophets | Through prophets |
| Human Nature | Equal ability to do good or bad | Two equal impulses, one good and one bad |
| Means of Salvation | Faith, good deeds | Faith, good deeds via the Five Pillars of Islam |

Despite the fundamental similarities between Judaism and Islam, most Jews around the world have a deeply distorted impression of Muslims. This is primarily because of what they've heard through rumors and badly written accounts of the infamous Battle of the Trench that took place near Medina in the seventh century. In almost every Western book or documentary film about Islam, varying interpretations of this event are mentioned. For that reason, I believe that it is necessary to provide the facts surrounding this notorious encounter. But not to burden the reader with too much detail, I've attempted to condense the sequence of events of this complicated siege into a few pages.

## THE INFAMOUS BATTLE OF THE TRENCH

The Battle of the Trench is also known as the Battle of the Confederates. The Quran uses the term "Confederates" (*al-Ahzab* in Arabic) to highlight the confederacy of polytheists and Jews against the Muslims that took place near Medina in the year 627.

As background, the Prophet arrived in Medina in 622 (the year of the hijra) with his followers who were given shelter by members of the indigenous community known as *al-Ansar* (the victors). He proceeded to set about the establishment of a pact known as the Constitution of Medina between the Muslims, al-Ansar, and three powerful Jewish tribes, in order to regulate the matters of governance of the small town, as well as the extent and nature of intercommunity relations. Conditions of the pact included boycotting the polytheist Quraysh tribe of Mecca, abstinence from extending any support to them, and assistance of one another if attacked anywhere in Arabia by a third party, as well as defending Medina in case of an enemy attack.[2]

When the Prophet arrived in Medina, he was hoping that one particular group would support him—the Jews. Muhammad was trying to befriend them and get them on his side because he knew that the Jews worshiped the same God, as reinforced in the Quran:

> *And do not contest*
> *the people of scripture,*
> *unless with what is better,*
> *except those of them*

> *who have been unjust:*
> *say, "We believe*
> *in what was revealed to us,*
> *and what was revealed to you;*
> *for our God and your God is one,*
> *to Whom we all acquiesce."* [3]

In a relationship-building effort, Muhammad ordered the Muslims to fast *Ashoura*, or the Passover, in honor of the Jews. The *qibla* (the direction the Muslims face in prayer) was initially toward Jerusalem, the same direction the Jews faced in prayer. Following the Jewish tradition, he also declared that all newborn Muslim males must be circumcised.

Al-Ansar (who converted to Islam in 622) received him with open arms, but the Jewish tribes of the small town and its surrounding agrarian areas refused to do so. From the day of his arrival, they looked at him with suspicion. When he began preaching Islam, most of the Jews became his opponents, questioning everything he said and did. No matter how hard he tried to convince them that he was a prophet of God, similar to Moses and Jesus, the Jews of Medina wouldn't open up to him. This was probably due to a fear and insecurity that Muslims would eclipse their economic prowess and prestige. Impeded by his peaceful nature, Muhammad didn't react to the hostility of the Jews. Rather, he continued to treat them kindly. Taking his inaction against them as a weakness, they made his life difficult. Yet, impressed by his gentle nature, some of the Jewish girls of Medina decided to become his wives' servants. The Jewish tribes didn't take the decision of these girls kindly, and they became even more aggressive toward Muhammad.

Despite their conduct, the Prophet never turned to violence against the Jews; instead, he openly embraced them and tried to conciliate them with kindness and generosity. According to a well-known report relayed in Muslim tradition, when Muhammad was in Mecca one of his neighbors was a man of Jewish descent who would deliberately urinate and empty his garbage in front of the Prophet's home on a daily basis as a sign of discontent. Despite this unkind ritual, Muhammad would always greet him with a smile when they saw one another in the streets of Mecca. One day, the Prophet found no garbage in front of his house, so he went over to the man's home to ask about him. He was told that the man had become ill. Muhammad then asked permission to enter the man's home and offer his prayers for healing.

According to a hadith relayed by al-Bukhari, another demonstration of the Prophet's spirit of interfaith respect narrates as follows: "A funeral procession passed in front of a group of Muslims, so they stood up. They were told that the funeral procession was of one of the inhabitants of the lands under the protection of Muslims. They said, 'A funeral procession passed in front of the Prophet and he stood up. When he was told that it was the coffin of a Jew, Muhammad said, "So what, was it not of a living soul?"'"[4] What Muhammad was saying is that we need to remember that the essence of all the great faiths is love and compassion.

In addition to some fifteen peaceful Judaic tribes, the three major Jewish clans in Medina were the Banu Nadir, Banu Qaynuqa, and Banu Qurayza. The Jews of Medina were rich and successful in their businesses—a formidable force in the region. Most of the Jewish tribes earned their living through commerce, date-farming, and jewelry-making. These three influential tribes are summarized as follows:

| THE MAJOR JEWISH TRIBES OF MEDINA | | |
|---|---|---|
| **BANU NADIR** | **BANU QAYNUQA** | **BANU QURAYZA** |
| After trying to assassinate the Prophet, they were exiled from Medina to an oasis town called Khaybar, approximately sixty miles northwest of Medina.<br><br>They initiated contact with the polytheist Quraysh tribe of Mecca in a confederacy to eliminate the Muslims. | When a Muslim woman visited a jeweler's shop in the Qaynuqa marketplace, she was aggressively pestered. The goldsmith, who was a Jew, pinned her clothing such that when getting up she was stripped naked. A Muslim man coming upon the resulting commotion killed the goldsmith in retaliation. The Jews in the marketplace, in turn, killed the Muslim man. This escalated into a chain of revenge-killings, and enmity grew between the Qaynuqa and the Muslims.<br><br>Following this incident, and for treason, they were exiled from Medina. | Lived close to Medina.<br><br>The Jewish tribe signed a pact with the Prophet, which they later broke. They were the strongest opponents to Muhammad and had tried to eliminate him.<br><br>After a disastrous twenty-five-day siege on Medina, some 700 of their men were executed for treason.<br><br>According to Arab tradition, the penalty for treason was clearly defined: the men were to be killed, the women and children sold into slavery, and their property distributed as booty. |

**Note:** Other tribes involved in the Battle of the Trench included the Arab Ghatafan, Aus, and Khazraj clans.

After their expulsion from Mecca, the Muslims fought the polytheist Meccans of Quraysh at the Battle of Badr in 624 and at the Battle of Uhud the following year.[5] Although the Muslims were defeated at Uhud, their strength was slowly growing, which was making the Quraysh anxious. Other wealthy tribes in Arabia that benefited from centuries of economic clout and political prestige, such as the three powerful

Jewish tribes of Medina, also started to feel threatened, even though the Muslims had never initiated any attacks against them.

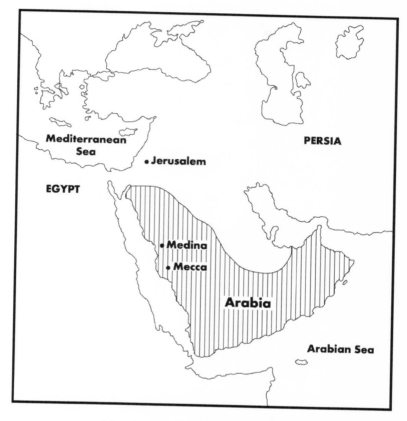

*Map 2. Arabia in the Seventh Century*

In early 627, the Jews of Nadir met with the Quraysh in Mecca to swear allegiance and to strategize a massive attack to eliminate Muhammad once and for all.[6] In total, the strength of the Confederate army, led by Abou Sufyan ibn Harb of

Quraysh, is estimated to have been more than ten thousand men, while the Muslim army consisted of only about three thousand soldiers.[7]

Once they knew that the Confederates were planning an attack, the Muslims opted to engage in a defensive battle by digging a deep trench to act as a barrier along the northern and eastern fronts of Medina.[8] Every capable Muslim, including Muhammad, contributed to digging a 5,500-meter-long trench in six days. The trench was dug on those two sides as the rest of Medina was surrounded by rocky lava-flow mountains and heavily treed areas impenetrable by large armies. Muhammad established his headquarters atop a hill called Sala to the north of Medina, overlooking the trench and giving the Muslims an advantage if the enemy crossed the dugout.

The siege on Medina began on March 31, 627, and lasted for twenty-five days.[9] The arriving Confederates were completely unprepared to deal with the trench dug by the Muslims, since such a defensive tactic had never before been implemented in Arabia. The Confederates initially attempted several simultaneous attacks on their own, but were unsuccessful, so they tried to persuade the Qurayza to attack the Muslims from the south. It was Huyay ibn Akhtab, the leader of the exiled Jewish tribe of Nadir, who sought the support of the Qurayza against the Muslims. So far, the Qurayza had tried to remain neutral and were hesitant to join the Confederates since they had an existing pact with Muhammad. The aggressive Huyay ibn Akhtab persuaded them that the Muslims would be overwhelmed if they opened a second front against them from the south, and tore into pieces the pact between the Qurayza and the Prophet.[10]

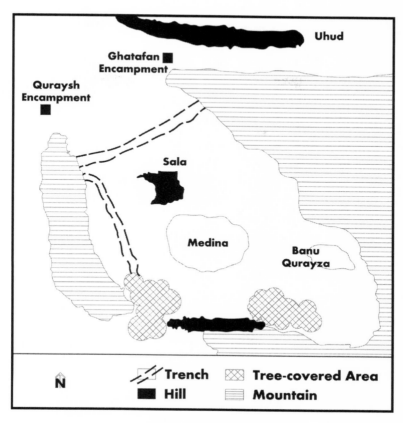

*Map 3. The Battle of the Trench*

News of the renunciation of their pact with Muhammad leaked. Because of his pact with the Qurayza, who possessed large numbers of weaponry, the Prophet hadn't made defensive preparations for the Jewish tribe along the Muslims' southern border.[11] Muhammad then sent three leading Muslims to bring back details of the recent developments. However, he cautioned against spreading the news of a possible breach of the pact on the Qurayza's part to avoid panic within the Muslim ranks. The leaders found that the pact had indeed been renounced and tried in vain to convince the Qurayza to revert by reminding them of the fates of the Nadir and the Qaynuqa, both exiled from Medina.[12]

Muhammad attempted to hide his knowledge of the treason of the Qurayza for the benefit of the Muslim soldiers. However, rumors soon spread of a massive assault on Medina designed to capture and torture the families of the Muslim soldiers. The Muslims found themselves in greater difficulties by the day. Food was running short and the nights were unusually cold for this time of year. So tense was the situation that, for the first time, the five daily prayers were neglected by the Muslim community. Only at night, when the attacks stopped due to darkness, did they resume their worship.[13]

The crisis showed Muhammad that many of his men had reached the limits of their endurance, so he had to act swiftly. He sent word to the Arab Ghatafan clan (which had come along with the Quraysh) to try to negotiate their defection, offering them a third of Medina's date harvest if they withdrew, which they agreed to. Before Muhammad began the order of drafting the agreement, and in democratic manner, he consulted several Medinan leaders. They rejected the terms of the agreement with the Ghatafan, protesting that they had never sunk to such levels of humiliation, so the negotiations were broken off.[14] Although the Ghatafan clan didn't retreat, they'd already compromised their position with the Confederates by entering into negotiations with the Prophet, resulting in an increase in the Confederacy's internal rifts.

At this point, and according to the historian Ibn Ishaq, the Prophet received a visit from Nuaym ibn Masud, an Arab leader who was respected by the Confederacy but had secretly converted to Islam. Muhammad pleaded with him to end the siege as soon as possible by creating discord among the Confederates. When ibn Masud asked permission to deceive, the Prophet, after having experienced trickery and treason from the Qurayza, replied, "Do what you can to draw the Confederates off from us—war is indeed deceit."[15]

Nuaym ibn Masud first went to the Qurayza and was able to warn them that if the siege failed, the Quraysh of Mecca wouldn't be afraid to abandon the Jews, leaving them at the mercy of the Muslim soldiers. Skillfully, Nuaym then went to Abou Sufyan (the Confederate leader), falsely warning him that the Qurayza had defected back to Muhammad. Numerous confused messages were repeatedly sent back and forth and further dissension and mistrust spread through the ranks of the Confederates and their allies. Amidst the confusion, Abou Sufyan summoned the Nadir leader, Huyay ibn Akhtab, and openly branded him as a traitor and tried to kill him.[16]

## DEFEAT OF THE CONFEDERATES

As mentioned earlier, the Arab Ghatafan clan had already been compromised by negotiations with Muhammad. They had taken part in the siege in hopes of plunder, rather than any particular hatred against Islam. They lost hope as the chances of victory dwindled, and retreated back to their village in the Najd desert. At this juncture, the provisions of the Confederate armies were starting to run out. Horses and camels were dying of hunger and wounds.[17] For days, the weather had been cold and rainy. Violent winds blew out their campfires, taking away their only source of heat. The Muslim camp, however, was sheltered from the strong winds. During the night, and after a disastrous twenty-five-day siege, the Confederate armies finally broke down and withdrew.

## FATE OF THE BANU QURAYZA

Following the retreat, the Qurayza strongholds were besieged by the Muslims, and their belongings and weapons were collected to be taken back to Medina. The men of Qurayza, numbering around seven hundred, were tied up and kept aside in a field.[18] The Jewish women and children were placed in the custody of Abdullah ibn Sallaam, a former rabbi who had converted to Islam.

The neutral Aus tribe of Medina immediately sent a delegation to the Prophet requesting him to deal with the Qurayza with the same clemency he had shown so far to other groups that had conspired against him in previous battles. In his typical democratic manner, Muhammad asked the Aus tribe, "Would you be satisfied if I asked one of you to pronounce the judgment about them?"[19] They all agreed unanimously.

The Prophet had so far spared all his prisoners' lives.[20] At the Battle of Badr in 624, some of the Quraysh captives who were among his fiercest enemies resurfaced once again at the subsequent Battle of Uhud at which the Muslims were heavily defeated. But after Badr, he had peacefully allowed the Quraysh to leave with their women, children, and possessions. The same happened with the Jewish Nadir after they betrayed their pact with Muhammad, with their chief, Huyay ibn Akhtab, later becoming one of the most deceptive leaders of the Confederates. Among the seven hundred captured Qurayza men, many were exiles from the Nadir tribe.

Therefore, his clemency had no effect on most of those who took advantage of it, and it sent a confusing message throughout Arabia during a time of rampant wars.[21] Muhammad, Arabs thought, never ordered the killing of prisoners, contrary to Arabian or even Jewish wartime customs at the time.[22] In their minds, his clemency was a sign of weakness, if not foolishness. Moreover, the treason of the Jewish Qurayza was so dire that if their plans had succeeded it would have easily led to the extermination of the Muslims.[23]

The neutral Aus tribe (not Muhammad) selected Saad ibn Muad, a respected figure in the Medina community who had previous ties with the Qurayza. Saad ibn Muad first wanted to make sure that his verdict would be respected by all, so he turned to the leaders of various groups, who, one by one, pledged to abide by his decision. He then addressed the Prophet, who, in wanting to keep the current events flowing, indicated that he wouldn't oppose Ibn Muad's decision either. Ibn Muad finally decided that the seven hundred men of the Qurayza should be executed, while the women and children would be considered as war captives.[24] Based on the democratic process already set in motion, and after consultation with his closest companions, Muhammad accepted the sentence, which was carried out by Muslim soldiers over the next few days.[25] It is beneficial to know that the Prophet did *not* execute any of the men of Qurayza, as is often claimed by biased Western observers.

### AFTERMATH OF THE BATTLE OF THE TRENCH

The news of the Muslim victory spread quickly throughout Arabia and drastically transformed perceptions and balances of power. Not only had the Muslims resisted the Confederate army of more than ten thousand men, they had shown unwavering determination and persistence. In addition, the fate of the men of Qurayza delivered a powerful message to all the neighboring tribes that tricks, treason, and aggression would, from that day forward, be punished. The message was received loud and clear—such a situation never occurred again during Muhammad's lifetime.[26]

The incident of the Qurayza was without doubt a dreadful event, but it would be a grave error to judge it by the standards of our own time. Arabia was still a primitive society that witnessed numerous atrocities and bloodbaths. The Muslims themselves had barely escaped extinction, and had Muhammad simply exiled the Qurayza, they would have quickly reignited the opposition and brought on another massive attack against the Muslims.[27] Additionally, in seventh-century Arabia, an Arab leader wasn't expected to show clemency to such traitors as the Qurayza. As such, the executions sent a bleak message to the Prophet's enemies and subdued the polytheist opposition throughout Arabia.[28]

Unfortunately, there are groups of Jews who still believe today that the events surrounding the Battle of the Trench are proof that Judaism is the enemy of Islam. In turn, there are groups of Muslims who continue to think that what happened in 627 is evidence that Jews are deceitful and untrustworthy. They are both wrong. The Battle of the Trench was a life-or-death situation in which survival instincts took over, an incident that was fueled primarily by political alliances and economic ties, not religious fervor or theological debates over scripture. The struggle didn't indicate any resentment toward Jews in general, but *only* toward the three tribes who wanted to kill the Prophet and who didn't seem to comprehend the meaning or significance of treaties. It was also an example of Muslims applying the self-defense rulings of Islam pertaining to warfare (referred to in chapter 6).

After this incident, the remaining tribes of Nadir and Qaynuqa migrated to Syria where they assimilated with the Jewish communities. Other, smaller Jewish tribes who were not involved in the Battle of the Trench continued to live peacefully in Medina, and later enjoyed full religious liberty under the Islamic Caliphate.[29] In addition, the verses of the Quran continued to venerate Jewish prophets (Aaron, David, Jacob, Moses, and Solomon) and urged Muslims to respect the People of the Book.

## ZIONISM

Zionism is a movement that was founded in 1896 by Theodor Herzl, whose goal was the return of Jews to Eretz Yisrael, or Zion, the Jewish synonym for Jerusalem and the Land of Israel. The term "Zionism" comes from Zion, the hill on which the Temple of Jerusalem was once situated.

In 1975, the General Assembly of the United Nations adopted a resolution declaring that "Zionism is a form of racism and racial discrimination." Zionism is also an extremist political ideology that's intertwined with radical Jewish teachings which Jews and others may accept or reject at will. There are many faithful Jews who are non-Zionists or even anti-Zionists, and an anti-Zionist posture doesn't necessarily mean that its holder is anti-Jewish. In fact, there are several Jewish organizations in the United States that openly condemn Zionism.[30]

## ANTI-SEMITISM

One of the consequences of Zionism is "anti-Semitism," a widely misused terminology in the Western lexicon. The Israeli historian Robert Wistrich has emphasized the problematic nature of the term "anti-Semitism," derived from a group of cognate "Semitic" languages (stemming from the Biblical Shem, one of Noah's three sons)—Arabic, Aramaic, Assyrian, Babylonian, Ethiopic, and Hebrew.[31] Wistrich explained that the term was incorrectly applied to a so-called racial designation that was coined by the German journalist Wilhelm Marr in the 1870s.[32] Wistrich also noted that "The illogical term 'anti-Semitism'...has come to be accepted in general usage as denoting all forms of hostility toward Jews and Judaism throughout history."[33] Therefore, the argument must be put forward that the Arabs and Arab-Muslims cannot be "anti-Semitic," because they themselves *are* Semites.

Anti-Judaism is essentially a Christian vice instigated after the Crusades when thousands of Jews were slaughtered along with numerous Muslims.[34] It's important to distinguish between anti-Jewish sentiment and anti-Zionism, because they are two completely different strands of bias. The dislike of Zionists, which is more politically driven than religion-related, became marked in the Muslim world only after the creation of the state of Israel in 1948, and the subsequent loss of mostly Arab-Muslim Palestine. Following the creation of Israel, a small percentage of Muslims was compelled to import anti-Zionist sentiment from Christian Europe and Russia, and translate into Arabic such potent (and allegedly forged) texts as the *Protocols of the Elders of Zion*. The importation of such texts was due to the fact that there were no similar Muslim-created texts ever written before.[35]

Because of the hostility toward Zionists, some Muslims incorrectly take verses from the Quran that refer to the Battle of the Trench completely out of context to justify their unfounded prejudice against Jews today. By taking such verses out of context, they're distorting both the message of the Quran and the attitude of the Prophet toward conflict—who himself had no hatred toward followers of the Jewish faith. That is, the misinterpretation of the Quran's verses by some radical Muslims, instigated by the creation of Israel and the protracted Israeli-Palestinian conflict, has reignited the myth that Judaism is the enemy of Islam.

Muslims don't hate Jews in general or even some Jews in particular. Rather, they dislike the politics and tactics of the Zionists that antagonize the innocent people of the occupied territories in Palestine, who want to live on their land alongside the Jews in peace and freedom.

## CONCLUSION

Judaism is a great religion that celebrates the one and only God—and Moses, one of the greatest prophets of all time, is highly revered throughout the Quran:

> *And mention Moses in the Book;*
> *he was one chosen, and was a messenger,*

*a prophet.*
*We called him*
*from the right side of Mount Sinai,*
*and We drew him near*
*to entrust a secret.*[36]

All through history, the Jews have contributed immensely to human civilization, whether through science, technology, art, music, or commerce. Tragically, Jews have experienced terrible suffering over the centuries because of envy, monstrous racism, and ignorance. As intelligent beings living in the twenty-first century, we need to move on and learn from the errors and horrors of the past—whether from the events surrounding the Battle of the Trench, in which an estimated seven hundred men were executed, or the two World Wars, in which more than seventy million people were killed.

Although the seemingly never-ending Israeli-Palestinian conflict is still unfolding, it shouldn't be linked to the myth that Judaism is the enemy of Islam. That's because it's a multilayered conflict that carries with it thousands of years of racial, political, and territorial strife. Christians and Muslims face a similar situation today because heinous historical events such as the Crusades continue to fuel the myth that Christianity is the enemy of Islam.

# MYTH EIGHT:

## Christianity Is the Enemy of Islam

Tensions have existed between Christianity and Islam for centuries, caused by a lack of knowledge and appalling events such as the Crusades. Despite historical tensions, Muslims bear great respect for Christians, as they are the followers of Jesus, the messenger who occupies an exalted position with God. In Islam, Jesus (*Eissa* in Arabic) is believed to be one of the greatest prophets of God to humankind. To reflect his elevated status in Islam, God revealed numerous verses in the Quran about him and his mother Mary.

For Muslims, Mary is an absolute symbol of submission to God and piety, and is considered *the* most righteous woman who has ever lived. Mary (*Maryam* in Arabic) is the only woman mentioned by name in the Quran. In fact, her name is mentioned more times in the Quran than in the New Testament. Significant events in the life of Jesus and his mother are explained lucidly in both "The Family of Amran" and "Mary" chapters of the Quran, as in the following verses:

*And God will teach him scripture*
*and wisdom, and the Torah and the Gospel,*
*and to be an emissary*
*to the Children of Israel:*
*"I [Jesus] have come to you with a sign from your Lord.*
*I will make you a figure of a bird out of clay,*
*and breathe into it,*
*whereat it will become a bird,*
*with God's permission.*
*And I heal the blind and the leprous,*
*and revive the dead,*
*with God's permission.*
*And I tell you what you consume*
*and what you keep in your homes."*
*Surely there is a sign in that for you,*
*if you are believers.*[1]

## THE CRUSADES

Roger Du Pasquier, the Swiss journalist and winner of the French Authors' Association Prize reports that "The West has never really known Islam. Ever since they watched it appear on the world stage, Christians never ceased to insult and slander it in order to find justifications for waging war on it."[2]

The most notorious wars waged against the Muslims were the Crusades. The Crusades originally had the goal of recapturing Jerusalem, the Holy Lands, and lucrative trade routes from Muslim rule, and were launched in response to a call from the Christian-Byzantine Empire for help against the expansion of the Muslim Seljuk-Turks into Anatolia (modern-day Turkey) in 1099.

Far from glorious, the Crusades were some of the bloodiest battles that the world has ever seen. Christians today wish that the Crusades could be taken back, because they have caused more harm to Christianity than any other action. The Crusades were basically a series of religiously sanctioned military campaigns waged by much of Latin-Christian Europe, particularly the Franks of France and the Roman Empire. The specific crusades to restore Christian control of Jerusalem and its surrounding Holy Lands were fought over a period of nearly 175 years, between 1099 and 1272. Nine in total, they were fought mainly against Muslims, yet campaigns were also waged against Jews in the Rhineland en route to Jerusalem.[3] As a result, crusading made anti-Judaism an incurable disease in Europe, and would also ineradicably blemish relations between Islam and the West.

Crusaders took vows and were granted automatic penance for past sins, therefore attracting hordes of social rejects, rapists, and murderers to their ranks. Their rampages were extremely brutal, especially when it came to the slaughtering of women and children. It's been conservatively estimated that at least thirty thousand Muslims were massacred during the Crusades.[4]

Elements of the Crusades were criticized from the time of their inception. For example, the English philosopher and

Franciscan friar Roger Bacon (d. 1294) felt that the Crusades were not effective, because "those who survive, together with their children, are more and more embittered against the Christian faith."[5] Later, eighteenth-century thinkers judged the Crusaders harshly. Some modern historians in the West also expressed moral outrage. The British historian Sir Steven Runciman (d. 2000) wrote a resonant condemnation: "High ideals were besmirched by cruelty and greed...the Holy War was nothing more than a long act of intolerance in the name of God."[6] As a result, in certain contexts a "crusade" is now a byword for aggression.

Some may argue that there's no need to dwell on the Crusades, as we must put the past behind us and learn from the mistakes of history, hoping that they'll never happen again. I can't agree more, but the reason I place the Crusades at the beginning of this chapter is to get them out of the way first—to simply highlight that, historically, Muslims did not brutally attack the Christians for any religious reasons. Rather, it was the other way round.

## The Similarities between Islam and Christianity

There are numerous similarities between the two great religions of Christianity and Islam. For example, both divine faiths believe that Jesus was sinless and infallible. Both religions accept that Jesus performed miracles and was supernaturally ascended (or raised up) to God. Both believe that God created humanity along with everything else, and that humankind has a superior place among all of His creations.

In addition, both religions teach that everything individuals earn isn't necessarily their own, so some of it should be given to the poor. For Christians, a tithe (from the Greek "tenth") of the income before taxes can be taken out and given to support their church and any other organizations their house of worship donates money to. For Muslims, 2.5 percent of a person's net annual income (after all debts and bills) is paid as mandatory charity and given to the poor.

Muslims pray five times a day. Without prayer, Muslims wouldn't be able to ritually praise God and thank Him for sending Abraham, Moses, Jesus, and Muhammad, and for revealing His scripture. In a similar way, Christians place prayer in high regard, praying at worship, often at daily devotions, and saying grace before meals. The idea of communicating with God is similar to the reasons of prayer for Muslims, enabling Christians to experience serenity and spiritual comfort. As Muslims fast during the month of Ramadan, Christians also believe in fasting for God; some Christians fast during the day for forty days, as Jesus is said to have done (Matthew 4:2).

## THE OPENING CHAPTER OF THE QURAN

The first chapter in the Quran is called "The Opening" (or *Al-Fatiha*), which is the most frequently recited chapter by Muslims. It's traditionally whispered into the right ear of a newborn baby as a welcoming gesture to this world; it's narrated before a couple is wed; it's required at the beginning of each of the seventeen daily prayer-cycles; and it's recited at funerals for the souls of the deceased. Al-Fatiha is believed by Muslims to encompass the essential teachings of God, condensed into one single chapter:

> *In the name of God,*
> *the Benevolent,*
> *the Merciful.*
> *Praise is proper to God,*
> *Lord of the universe,*
> *the Benevolent,*
> *the Merciful,*
> *Ruler of the day of judgment.*
> *It is You we serve,*
> *to You we turn for help.*
> *Show us the straight path,*
> *the path of those You have favored,*
> *not of those who are objects of Your anger,*
> *nor of those who wander astray [from God].*[7]

The translation that's provided above by Thomas Cleary is accurate and reflects the principal teachings of Islam.[8] But, unfortunately, if you pick up some poorly translated Qurans, you'll find the following translation of the last two lines of Al-Fatiha: "*Not the way of those who earned Your anger, such as the Jews, nor of those who went astray, such as the Christians.*"

If a group of Muslims in, say, Egypt or Saudi Arabia, are asked who "*not of those who are objects of Your anger, nor of those who wander astray*" is referring to, they'll probably respond, "The Jews and the Christians." If you ask them, "And who said so?" they'll likely tell you, "It's in the Quran," or simply, "The Prophet did." This is actually one of the biggest inter-faith blunders, which many Muslims have been committing for centuries, and continue to do today. This is a situation wherein religious ignorance by Muslims themselves contributes to the myth that Christianity is the enemy of Islam. To change this dismal reality, one would hope that more and more Muslims do their own research and discover that what has been ingrained in their minds since childhood by warped interpretations and religious folklore is wrong.

First of all, there are no strong hadith supporting that Muhammad ever said that the last two lines of the Al-Fatiha refer to the Jews and the Christians. In fact, the Prophet never directly deciphered the verses of the Quran because he knew that God wanted most of its interpretation to be flexible for all times. Logic dictates that the verse is referring to all people, *including* Muslims, who derail from the straight path of righteousness. Second of all, if the Quran intended to refer to the Jews and the Christians, it would have indicated so directly.

In a similar vein, it should be noted that non-Muslims are not called "infidels" in Islam as is commonly thought by Western observers. All the members of the divine religions—Jews, Christians, and Muslims—are called "believers." We may have different beliefs in our religions, but we all believe in the same God—we simply know God in different ways.

In Islam, only the nonbelievers are called "blasphemers," but they should be treated the same as Muslims. There's no verse in the Quran that orders the ill-treatment of blasphemers. To the contrary, Muslims are ordered to treat them fairly and try to be role models to help them see the good values that Islam can offer.

Above all, Muslims don't hate Christians. Hate doesn't exist in Islam, especially against people of other faiths, including Hindus and Buddhists. The Quran teaches Muslims to have sympathy toward all humans, without any discrimination due to religion or color.

### ISLAMIC AND CHRISTIAN SCRIPTURE

The Quran highlights the broad relationships among the divine scriptures, as in the following verse:

> *God revealed the Book to you in truth,*
> *verifying what was before it;*
> *God revealed the Torah and the Gospel before*
> *as guidance for all humanity.*[9]

Western readers with some knowledge of the biblical narratives may be inspired by the frequent mentioning in the Quran of familiar stories of Adam and Eve, Abraham, Moses, David and Solomon, and Jesus and Mary. However, upon closer examination of the scriptures—such as the comparison of the story of Joseph in chapter 12 of the Quran with the account in Genesis (37–50)—inevitable questions are raised by Muslims and non-Muslims alike. When Christians read in the Quran about Moses or Joseph, Jesus or Mary—who say and do things somewhat differently than in the biblical narratives—they conclude that the Quran has to be a "corrupted borrowing."[10] Muslims, in turn, explain these discrepancies as evidence that Christians have modified the original revelations of Jesus to make their religion more "attractive." Actually, it's argued by some that had the earlier People of the Book not altered the record, God wouldn't have needed to restore His revelation by sending Muhammad a corrective message.[11] Of course, neither point of view is productive, for both conclusions arise more out of a skewed sense of "monotheistic competition" and insecurity than out of a sincere desire to openly analyze the data of history.[12] The arguments seek only to defend the integrity of one scripture at the expense of the other, which at the end of the day doesn't get us anywhere.

To resolve this dilemma, we must take the macro view of God's communication with humanity. For example, Christians might want to explore this quandary from the following perspective: as stories of the primary religious figures don't belong exclusively to any people, their capacity to reveal the divine truth belongs to all whom God wishes their access to be granted.[13] In other words religious stories are the possession of *all* humanity. Besides, if variations on specific narratives that some associate with the Bible occur in the Quran, they are there for an important purpose that transcends the "rights" of Christians to claim exclusive ownership of "their" stories and truths.[14] As for their part in solving the dilemma, Muslims must view the Quran as bringing a new perspective, reinforcing the previous messages and updating the opportunities for all willing people to worship and experience God equally. Muslims also need to come to terms with the fact that because Christians have different religious traditions, it doesn't mean that they are wrong, and vice versa.

## Islam's View of Jesus

Islam views Jesus as a great prophet who came to convey an authentic message of love and compassion. Muslim teaching asserts that the *Injil*, or the prophetic gospel originally delivered by Jesus, has for various reasons been changed over the course of Christian transmission.[15] Consequently, Muslims believe that little reliance can be placed on the majority of text in the Christian tradition (including the four canonical Gospels of the New Testament—Matthew, Mark, Luke, and

John) as representing the *original* teachings of Jesus. However, Muslim scholars are enthused by the specific elements of one of the various gospels known as the Gospel of Barnabas that supposedly concurs with Quranic teachings, such as the denial of Jesus as being the divine son of God. But why is it that Muslims don't believe that Jesus is the son of God? It's primarily because of the following chapter in the Quran, named "Pure Truth":

> *Say, "It is God, unique,*
> *God the eternal,*
> *not begetting or begotten,*
> *not having any equal."* [16]

Most Muslims would say that this chapter is an embodiment of the whole Quran—the establishment of the oneness of God. The underlying message from "Pure Truth" in relation to Jesus is that if God is "not begetting," then Jesus cannot be His divine son in a literal sense. The logic of this chapter can also be taken a step further: if Jesus is God (or the direct manifestation of God on earth) as is believed by Christians, then how could Jesus worship God? In the Book of Consolation of Second Isaiah (45:21), quite a similar description of God (*Yahweh* in old Hebrew) is conveyed:

No God was formed before Me,

nor will be after Me.

I, I am Yahweh,

there is no other God but me.[17]

As such, Muslims don't believe that Jesus is the divine son of God. Rather, Muslims believe that he was a human prophet and not in any way divine himself.

Based on the following verses wherein Jesus is described as having a profoundly intimate dialogue with God, the Christian messenger himself is conveying that he never claimed to be divine:

> *And if God asks:*
> *"Jesus, Son of Mary, did you tell people,*
> *'Take to me and my mother as deities*
> *rather than God'?"*
> *Jesus will reply, "Glory to You.*
> *It is not for me to say what I have no right to.*
> *If I used to say that, You would have known it.*
> *You know what is in my essence,*
> *while I do not know what is in Your essence.*
> *For you are the one*
> *who knows all hidden secrets.*
> *I never told them anything*
> *but what You instructed me—'Worship God,*
> *my Lord and your Lord.'"* [18]

The Quran also conveys the prediction by Jesus of the arrival of Muhammad after him. The Arabic name "Ahmad," as mentioned below, is actually another name for "Muhammad" (which means "the highly praised" or "the one who constantly thanks God").

> *And Jesus Son of Mary said:*
> *"O Children of Israel, I am God's messenger to you,*
> *confirming the truth of the Torah before me,*
> *and heralding a messenger*
> *who will come after me,*

*his name Ahmad, most praiseworthy. "*
*But when Jesus brought them proofs, they said,*
*"This is obvious sorcery. "* [19]


## THE COUNCIL OF NICAEA

The Council of Nicaea was a gathering of Christian bishops convened in Nicaea, Bithynia (present-day Turkey), in 312 by the Roman Emperor Constantine I.[20] Constantine had been a leader in a cult known as *Sol Invictus* (or "Invincible Sun") and wanted to unite the various Christian sects in the Roman Empire under his existing pagan church, the Universal Church of Rome. Constantine had adopted Christianity as the "state religion" because he was seeking something powerful that would unite the masses of his vast empire; however, in his view, a heresy had developed which threatened to dissolve that desired unity, and Constantine wouldn't allow it. The heresy was caused by Arius of Alexandria (d. 336) who was teaching that Jesus, instead of being fully divine, as was believed by Christians, was a human being.[21] As a result, Arianism was condemned at the Council, and Arius was exiled by Constantine, who intended to make sure that, one way or another, these disagreements would end.

The Council was historically significant as the first effort to attain consensus through an assembly representing all of Christendom. The Council was also of major significance because it established the groundwork for the following new beliefs for Christianity:[22]

1. "We believe in one God, the Father Almighty, maker of all things visible and invisible,

2. and in one Lord, Jesus Christ, the Son of God, the only-begotten of the Father, that is, of the substance of the Father, God of God, light of light, true God from true God, begotten not made, of one substance with the Father,

3. by whom all things were made, those things that are in heaven and those things that are on earth,

4. who for us men and for our salvation came down and was made man,

5. he suffered, rose again on the third day, then ascended into the heavens,

6. and will come again to judge the living and the dead.

7. And we believe in the Holy Spirit."

Other significant developments that resulted from the Council of Nicaea and the subsequent Council of Constantinople in 381 (which collectively became known as the Nicene Creed[23]) include:

♦ Declaring that disbelief in the Trinity is a heresy;

♦ Changing the Christian day of worship from Saturday to Sunday (to be different from the Jewish Sabbath);

♦ Establishing the date of Jesus's birthday as December 25 (to mirror the pagan feast of the son of Isis, the ancient Egyptian goddess of nature);

♦ Introduction of Easter (derived from the pagan "Feast of Ishtar"); and

♦ The Church of Rome officially became the "Universal Church of the Holy Roman Empire" (the word "Universal" actually means "Catholic").[24]

As presented, the Councils of Nicaea and Constantinople fundamentally changed the future course of Christianity, as well as the original teachings of Jesus (known in Arabic as the Injil) which Islam is in harmony with. As mentioned earlier, the Quran indicates that Jesus didn't say that he was the divine son of God, or even God Himself. To the contrary, he knew that he was a prophet similar to Abraham, Moses, and Muhammad who had a monotheistic message to convey for the betterment of all humanity. To that end, Christianity is not the enemy of Islam, because Muslims fully believe in Jesus and his original teachings. But Islam doesn't concur with the numerous changes implemented through the Nicene Creed, especially the notion of the Trinity, which is denied in 5:73 of the Quran:

*Those who say God*
*is one third of a trinity*
*have certainly blasphemed,*
*for there is no deity but one God.*


## THE CRUCIFIXION OF JESUS

Christians believe that Jesus literally died on a cross around the year 30. On the other hand, Muslim tradition accepts as true that Jesus wasn't crucified, because the Quran indicates that he didn't actually die on a cross. In this instance (as with the complex notion of the Trinity), what is taught in the Quran is somewhat different from what is taught in the New Testament. The Quran references the crucifixion of Jesus directly in the following verses:

*And on the account of their saying,*
*"We killed the Messiah Jesus,*
*Son of Mary, messenger of God,"*
*whereas they did not kill him,*
*they did not crucify him,*
*although it was made to seem thus to them.*
*As for those who differ on this,*
*they are certainly in doubt about it.*
*They have no accurate knowledge about it,*
*only following conjecture;*
*but they surely did not kill him:*
*rather God raised him*
*up to the divine presence;*
*and God is almighty, most wise.*[25]

Though the Quran doesn't expressly say so, the interpretation of most Muslims is that Jesus was "replaced" by another man, and that this other man (possibly Simon of Cyrene or an apostle) was the one crucified, not Jesus himself.[26] However, it is possible that these Quranic verses could be interpreted in different ways—that is, either literally or symbolically.

## CONCLUSION

Christianity is a beautiful religion that brings out the best in people, celebrating the love of God and neighbor, from which Islam has derived many of its teachings. But because Islam's scripture came after that of Christianity, the Quran is able to address the similarities and the various differences with Christians directly. That's why the Islamic understanding of the connections between the divine faiths is believed to be highly developed. On the other hand, some Muslims may assume to know "true" Christianity better than the Christians themselves. This is the wrong approach to take, as it makes the followers of Jesus feel threatened, especially when accompanied by a sense of self-righteousness on the part of Muslims.

It's quite clear that bad communication enhances religious misunderstanding, and that the pains of one generation are easily passed on to the next; therefore, Muslims and Christians face the challenge of improving communication with each other. Both faiths must focus on the promotion of educational attempts that are designed to break down biases and stereotypes. Moreover, Christians and Muslims must not consign each other to the anonymity of a mass humanity labeled "all Muslims" or "all Christians."[27]

The most-needed approach today is the mutual respect of doctrinal similarities *and* differences, a delicate matter of acknowledging built-in theological positions that can easily prejudice interfaith dialogue,[28] in particular the Christian view of its revelation as being "final" and the Muslim view that the once-pure message at the heart of Christianity was altered with the Synoptic Gospels, and is in need of reform and rewording.

Most Muslims believe that Christians need to reconnect with the essence of their original revelations. This is because Christianity, in its original form, was at some point identical to the basic teachings of Islam (i.e., *before* the establishment of the Nicene Creed). Granted, there are some theological variances between Christianity and Islam, but Muslims need to move beyond the minutiae of conflicting scripture, and not get too bogged down by such quandaries as the divinity of Jesus and whether he was actually crucified or not. As long as nobody is harmed by such differing beliefs, and if Christians attain spiritual comfort through their own views on the meaning of the life of Jesus, then Muslims should gracefully accept that perspective without a "holier-than-thou" attitude. Muslims also need to know that various sects of Christians are already implementing changes to bring Christianity back to its original pre-Nicene Creed teachings, namely the United Methodist Church in the US.

We all feel threatened when our fundamental beliefs are questioned or negated, so the need for patience in dialogue, cultural sensitivities, and the letting go of the desire to see the other change must be adopted. At the end of the day, it isn't about winning or losing, but about acknowledging our flawed humanity, and increasing mutual understanding and respect.

Islam is about inclusion, community, and tolerance. As such, the long-term goal should be to foster genuine openness, circumventing the threats of our religious differences and the realization by all that Christianity is *not* the enemy of Islam, or vice versa. Perhaps the best guided principle to follow is in the words of the Muslim mathematician-poet Omar Khayyam in his humbling confession of faith, written more than nine hundred years ago:

"Both you and I are born alike.
Though some may sink and some may soar,
we all are earth and nothing more."

# MYTH NINE:

## Islam Is Incompatible with Western Modernity

Much has been written on the subject of Islam and Western modernity. Part of it—without doubt—is outstanding, but part of it comes across as excessively defensive and written with a religious zeal that most people can't relate to, especially Western readers. On the other hand, and in my opinion, many Western observers believe that Islam is a backward-thinking religion that is engaged in ideological warfare with the West. This has widened the gap of misunderstanding and has further fortified the myth that Islam is incompatible with the Western world. As a result, there are many minds today that are agitated by, in the words of historian Samuel Huntington, a "clash of civilizations" between Islam and the West.

The question of Islam's compatibility with Western modernity can be approached from one of three positions:

1. Islam must adapt itself to modernity by eliminating all its beliefs and practices that are incompatible with modernity;
2. Islam rejects all modernist principles that are inconsistent with its teachings; or
3. Islam and modernity are mutually compatible and reconcilable.

I shall adhere to the third approach, discussing how a society can be both Islamic *and* adopt the general criteria of Western modernity. I've chosen the third approach because Islam provides all the necessary tools to help the Muslim world attain the prosperity of the West by the same methods the West has used, and because that can be achieved without endangering the essential values of Islam.

## WESTERN MODERNITY

By nature, humans are flawed and imperfect. An ideal society, therefore, is impossible to attain. However, we have to be optimistic, focusing on the positive aspects of modernity and constantly striving to adopt its better nature and best practices.

Western modernity can be characterized by several sacrosanct and nonnegotiable traits, namely, democracy, the respect of the rule of law, and the respect of human rights and the rights of free speech and gender equality. Other hallmarks of Western modernity include science and technology, the incessant quest for knowledge, the ethic of hard work, efficiency, and personal responsibility. These best practices, which are all heralded and taught by Islam, have evolved throughout the West since the Enlightenment period of the eighteenth century, when reason was becoming the backbone of human existence in Europe. By the twentieth century, the West had found it necessary to separate religion from politics in order to free government and science from the limitations of conservative religion.

At the same time, Western modernity can suggest electronic gadgets, conspicuous consumption, instant gratification, egotistical individualism, and an obsession with brand names. Unfortunately, horrific events such as the two World Wars have revealed the terrifying efficiency of modernity, when science and technology displayed their lethal potential. Military technology—which serves the interests of weapons corporations, arms dealers, and the national ego—is constantly lusting for absolute and objective certainty, despite the fact that human certainty is tantalizingly unattainable.

## WESTERN MODERNITY AND ISLAM

The Prophet Muhammad once said, "The attainment of knowledge is a must for every Muslim."[1] Furthermore, the relation between the Quran and science is strongly affirmed in Islamic thought. Almost all sources, classical and modern, agree that the Quran encourages science and the pursuit of knowledge. The text of the Quran is filled with verses inviting people to use their intellect, to ponder, to think, and to know. The Quran also says that there is no limit to learning, and that it is through the acquisition of knowledge and the use of reason that societies will prosper. The first word revealed to Muhammad via the Angel Gabriel was, after all, "Read!"

*Read, in the name of your Lord...*
*the one who taught the use of the pen,*
*taught man what he did not know.*[2]

Therefore, it isn't true that Islam is a barrier toward the creation of a modern, knowledge-based secular society, as biased Western observers often claim.

It's important to reemphasize the early Muslim passion for knowledge between 800 and 1200 (as discussed in chapter 5), because too many Westerners view Islam as being inherently closed-minded, medieval, and fervently opposed to modernity. To the contrary, Islam is a universal religion that insists on the importance of science and all kinds of advances that improve the quality of lives. It is for this reason that during early Islamic history Muslim scholars contributed enormously to philosophy, science, mathematics, the humanities, art, and architecture. It goes without saying that Andalusia, Baghdad, and Cairo were once the seats of world learning until their centers of education, scholars, and libraries fell prey to foreign destruction in the thirteenth century. It is also well-recognized that the Muslim scholars, with their accumulated knowledge from the earlier Greek, Hindu, and Chinese civilizations, had sowed the seeds of the sixteenth-century Renaissance which led to the European Enlightenment.

## ISLAMIC FUNDAMENTALISM

With the rise of political and military power, decadence and corruption inevitably spread within Muslim society, especially during the oppressive Ottoman Empire. In addition, due to the brutal European colonization of nearly all Islamic countries in the nineteenth and first half of the twentieth centuries (which was followed by numerous wars with Israel), Muslims stopped interacting with the wider world, and the rot set in. It was a result of this situation that an ultra-conservative religious class grew, eventually becoming inward-looking, with a narrow worldview. Religious clerics became wrapped in a sense of self-righteousness, and the virus of Islamic fundamentalism spread rapidly due to the likes of Hassan el-Banna (d. 1949) and Sayyid Qutb (d. 1966), the founders of extremism in Egypt. The sentiment of Muslims living under the oppression of fundamentalists can be felt through the sobering words of the Iranian poet, Saadi of Shiraz (d. 1287), who wrote:

"I am a dreamer who is mute,
and the people are deaf.
I am unable to say,
and they are unable to hear."

The rise of politically motivated Islamic fundamentalism has caused significant socioeconomic problems for many countries, namely Egypt, Pakistan, and Afghanistan. The unswerving literal interpretation of religious scripture and fundamentalism are rooted in profound fear and the paranoia of annihilation. That's probably why Muslim fundamentalists fear and reject Western modernity, assuming that their worldview is being erased in what they see as an ideological struggle for world domination. Their fundamentalism is also a reaction to their own inability, or unwillingness, to adapt to Western modernity.

The extremists' argument is that it's arrogant of the Western world to assume that its beliefs and ideas are the correct ones, while those of the Islamic world are incorrect. The fundamentalists also ask, "What gives any one system the right to impose its *modus vivendi* throughout a multicultural world?" But fundamentalists tend to focus only on the negative traits of Western modernity, retrenching themselves into a myopic worldview. Moderate Muslims, being the vast majority, have, on the other hand, a much more practical outlook as they usually query, "How can we take the best of Western modernity and blend it with Islamic values for the benefit of our societies?"

The blame that the extremists lay on Western modernity for the dire problems in the Muslim world is a simple excuse. It's much easier than examining the multilayered sociopolitical issues and grievances that have reverberated throughout much of the Muslim world. These problems have ranged from high unemployment, overpopulation, and income inequality to oppression and rampant corruption by dictatorial regimes. The majority of Muslim countries have experienced a lack of economic growth which, combined with exponentially growing populations and illiteracy, has resulted in widespread domestic discontent. This discontent has too often been channeled into Islamic fundamentalism because the masses have lost hope in their governments that pretend to apply democracy. Fundamentalism is not only an irrational blaze of behavior; it is misguided dissent.

One cannot blame the majority of Muslims who are illiterate or have low annual incomes for the multitude of problems in their countries. The fault partially lies with the dictatorial regimes that manipulated the wealth of their countries for their own protection and the protection of their "support system," comprised of wealthy business individuals, red-tape-government, the military, and the police. Some of the blame can also be placed on the humiliating colonization by European nations such as England, France, and Italy, which oppressed the psyche, national identity, and hopes of several generations of Muslims, many of whom are still alive today.

As a result, the Islamic world has a plethora of extremely complex problems caused by numerous factors that have been accumulating for centuries. These problems forced many Muslims to migrate to the West to seek a better future in what can be described as a massive brain drain. There are millions of Muslims all over the world living in Westernized cities and working in highly sophisticated technological, scientific, and financial fields. The majority of these Muslims have found a practical and balanced way to reconcile their faith with Western modernity.

However, it's the intolerant interpretation of their faith that a minority of Muslims choose to follow that is incompatible with modern society. It is unfortunate that this fanatical sect seems to be more successful at communicating their message than the silent majority. This fanatical sect is comprised of ultra-conservative Muslims who believe that the world we live in today should be as it was some 1,400 years ago. They reject the overall modus vivendi of Western modernity and tend to get caught up in irrelevant debates about distorted views on the applicability of Islam in modern society. For example, they debate whether men should have long or trimmed beards, if women should wear a niqab that shows one eye or two eyes, whether a mobile telephone should be held in the right hand or the left hand, if men are allowed to wear the traditional Arabian dress worn during the days of the Prophet up to the knees or below the knees, and so on.

It's this kind of self-absorbed guesswork and backwardness that's contributing to the current down-cycle that Islam's facing today, which the extremists blame on the West. Instead of wasting valuable time debating such frivolous matters, why not discuss ways to eradicate illiteracy and poverty, or debate how women's rights can be improved in Muslim countries?

## MUSLIMS IN THE WEST

In the United States, I have found that the educational background of most Muslim immigrants tends to have a significant impact on how they interpret and apply their faith, and how they interact with their surrounding communities. That is, the better the education, the wider the worldview and willingness to adapt to the best practices of Western modernity. By no means do I want to sound elitist or simplistic, yet it adds up, because along with a lack of knowledge and proper education comes myopic religious ignorance and intolerance. This is most evident during Ramadan when Muslims get together to end the fast at sunset and have lengthy discussions about the state of politics, society, and religion in the US and elsewhere in the West. At these gatherings, I've also observed that the older generation of Muslim immigrants in America tends to be introverted and insular compared to younger American-Muslims. These young Muslims are much more open-minded and interactive with people of different faiths and backgrounds, and are fluent in such social media as Facebook and Twitter. This is promising, because the more Muslims integrate and blend with the best practices of Western culture (while still maintaining their core Islamic values), the better off they will be economically in the West.

The same applies to the older religious clerics (*imams*) who preach Islam in the US. When I travel, I do my best to attend the required Friday prayer and sermon in a mosque. I'm often saddened by the poor level, or complete lack, of English spoken by the imams. In addition, some of them tend to focus on subjects that are already well known to Muslims, such as the macabre scenes of torture in the grave for sinners after death, hell, and the afterlife, in lieu of topics that would be more applicable for Muslims with pressing issues to deal with in their hectic daily lives. I realize that such hectoring is probably present in some synagogues and churches in the US, but Muslim imams must be able to present an up-to-date image of Islam to improve its negative perception in the West. One of the basic ways to achieve this is by communicating in understandable English, especially for the non-Arabic-speaking Muslims who attend Friday prayers. Islam in America needs more of the likes of the youthful Hamza Yusuf of the Zaytuna College or the well-educated Muzammil Siddiqi, the imam of the Islamic Society of Orange County in southern California. After all, in today's media-driven world, perception *is* reality.

Islam doesn't oppose Western modernity, and it isn't, by any means, opposed to, say, democracy, nuclear energy, space travel, electronic gadgets, or the Internet. But Islam opposes what it views as disrespectful culture, such as sexually arousing attire in public and promiscuous relationships outside marriage. Such behavior is not only prohibited, but can easily destroy families—the foundation of Islamic society.

A modernity that asks for a sacrifice of moral and ethical values is unacceptable in Islam. As such, the West has to respect Islamic values, and Islam must respect Western differences. This basic "live-and-let-live" approach is paramount for the success of future generations of Muslims in the West.

## ARAB-MUSLIMS AND WESTERN MODERNITY

The "Arab world" refers to Arabic-speaking countries—from the Atlantic Ocean in the west to the Arabian Sea in the east; from the Mediterranean in the north to the Indian Ocean in the southeast. It comprises twenty-two countries and territories with a combined population of 358 million people who include Muslims, Christians, and Jews.

Arab-Muslims in the Middle East and North Africa are constantly in the Western media's limelight. Although Arabs comprise only 20 percent of the world's Muslim population, they usually get the most attention from the West when it comes to religion and socioeconomic problems. That is because of their geographical proximity to Israel, a staunch ally of the US and many influential European nations, as well as the vast oil reserves in such countries as Saudi Arabia, Kuwait, and Iraq. So when something is wrong in the Arab Middle East, we instantly hear about it in the West—most often in a negative light.

Unfortunately, many things are wrong in Arab-Muslim countries that must be understood. Something is definitely not right when a small country such as Belgium, with a population of about ten million people, publishes more books every year than all the twenty-two nations of the Arab world combined, which have 358 million people.[3] Barely three hundred books a year are translated into Arabic, only a fifth as many translated by Greece for its eleven million citizens.[4]

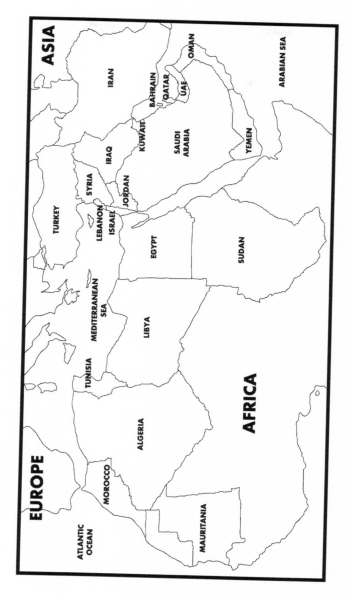

*Map 4. North Africa and the Middle East*

Illiteracy, which is rooted in colonization policy—particularly from the French and British—is endemic throughout the Arab Middle East. Then, too, is the failure to utilize the talents of half the population of the region, its women. The result of this leaves the combined gross domestic product (GDP) of all twenty-two nations of the Arab Middle East (excluding Israel) totaling some $530 billion, less than the GDP of Spain alone.[5] Only Turkey, whose founder Mustafa Kemal Ataturk had turned that nation's gaze to the West in the 1920s, has escaped this dismal fate. Turkey's secularism, a break from religious clerical control, was (and continues to be) backed up by a well-educated and progressive society.

It's vital to realize that these dire statistics are not the fault of Islam *itself*, because the Muslim faith provides all the necessary tools for success in life. The troubled modern history of the Arab Middle East is partially caused by most Muslims deviating from the basic teachings of the Quran and the Prophet Muhammad, and by the incorrect application of their own religion. That is, the application of honesty and integrity in their day-to-day dealings, personal accountability, and a "live conscience" are for the most part absent today, coupled with other factors which are reiterated below.

- ◆ Blanket colonization in the nineteenth and first half of the twentieth centuries
- ◆ The rise of Islamic fundamentalism and its myopic worldview
- ◆ Arcane ways of thinking that need urgent reform
- ◆ Corrupt governments and monarchies
- ◆ Blurred lines between the public and the private interests

- Dire socioeconomic problems such as endemic illiteracy which has caused backwardness, religious ignorance, and defective standards
- Numerous wars in the region, such as the Arab-Israeli conflict (from 1948 to the present), the Gulf War (1990–1991) and the Iraq War (2003–2010), that have drained the treasuries of numerous Arab countries
- An often fatalistic approach to life that tends to blame others for problems and misfortunes

### CULTURAL DIFFERENCES

There are several unfounded phobias in the West about Islam, due to the differences in religious traditions when compared to the Western modus vivendi. That is, differences in dress; ablution for prayer; animal sacrifice; the prohibition of alcohol, gambling, and pork; fasting; and Islamic finance. (The Arabic language barrier was discussed in chapter 2). As such, some Western observers claim that Islam and Western modernity are not compatible partially because of these different practices, which is incorrect because they are harmless and beneficial for Muslims.

As to the issue of dress, it's not uncommon to see groups of men from Pakistan or Afghanistan wearing their traditional attire in cities such as London and Los Angeles. But their dress code has nothing to do with Islam. It happens to be that they are Muslims who come from countries where the male masses wear their traditional turbans and flowing, Arabian-style attire. Although the English word "turban" comes from Persian, wearing the turban is an old tradition that originated in Arabia to deter dust and was later spread by the Arabs through trade. It is worth noting that Sikhs, who are not Muslims, also wear a turban as a distinct symbol of their identity, and for that reason are occasional victims of misguided discrimination in the West. (Chapter 4 provides a detailed discussion of women's rights and why women in Islam are encouraged to wear a veil).

Ablution (*wudu*) is the Islamic act of washing parts of the body (the face, hands, arms, and feet) using water. Muslims are required to be clean in preparation for their five daily prayers because the Quran says, "*God loves those who turn to Him, and He loves those who keep themselves pure and clean.*"[6] This focus on cleanliness was a major factor in the introduction of sanitation and bathing in many of the countries that Islam spread to, such as Spain.

Financially able Muslims are encouraged to purchase an animal during the Festival of Sacrifice (*Eid al-Adha*), which is also the time of the hajj (pilgrimage to Mecca). Usually a sheep or a goat is sacrificed in commemoration of God's forgiveness of Abraham from his vow to sacrifice his son Ishmael. This action is often misunderstood by those outside of Islam. The meat from the sacrifice is mostly given away to others: one-third can be eaten by immediate family and relatives, one-third given away to friends, and one-third donated to the poor—although the most common practice today is to distribute it all to the poor. This act of sacrifice symbolizes the willingness of Muslims to give up things that are of benefit to them or close to their hearts in order to follow God's commands.

Alcohol and gambling are prohibited in Islam because the Quran clearly cautions against such vices that can have an adverse impact on one's health and income, and because they place obstacles in the way to God:

> *They ask you about alcohol and gambling.*
> *Say, "There is great sin in them,*
> *and also advantages for people;*
> *but their sin is greater than their advantage."*[7]

Gambling can also easily wreck families and incomes, and become an addiction that's extremely hard to beat. So why start gambling in the first place? There's a saying in Arabic, "Avoid sin and sing to it from afar," meaning that one should try to happily avoid addictive temptations such as alcohol and gambling for a better, healthier way of life.

Fasting during the month of Ramadan (which is discussed in detail in chapter 1) is incorrectly viewed in the West as being "strange"—further fueling the myth that Islam is incompatible with Western modernity. Although fasting is beneficial for one's health, it's regarded principally as a method of self-purification. By detaching oneself from worldly comforts and pleasures, even for a short time, the fasting person achieves sympathy with those who go hungry, as well as a growth in spirituality. Fasting also teaches Muslims self-control, as mentioned in 2:183 of the Quran:

> *Fasting is prescribed for you,*
> *as it was prescribed for those before you*
> *[the Jews and Christians],*
> *that you may learn self-restraint.*

Lastly, Muslims (like Jews) are not allowed to eat pork. The Book of Deuteronomy (14:8, American King James Version) says, "And the swine, because it does not chew the cud, it is unclean for you: you shall not eat of their flesh, nor touch their dead carcass." Similarly, the Quran (2:173) cautions,

> *God has only forbidden you the carcass*
> *of a dead animal,*
> *and blood, and the flesh of the swine...*
> *But there is no transgression or blame*
> *on those who are compelled by necessity,*
> *without wanting to or going too far.*
> *For God is most forgiving, most merciful.*

### ISLAMIC FINANCE

There is a lingering phobia in the West that Islamic finance will one day take over the global capital markets through some kind of "holy financial jihad." That, of course, is ludicrous. As fear stems from ignorance, I shall attempt to explain the background of Islamic finance in the context of Western modernity, as well as its virtues.

Islamic finance started as a small cottage industry in Dubai in 1975.[8] It distinguishes itself from conventional finance in its ostensible compliance with principles of Islamic law, or sharia. Its growth has been accelerating ever since, in terms of the number of countries in which it operates, as well as the areas of finance into which it has ventured. In recent years, the industry has attracted a number of global financial institutions, such as Citigroup, HSBC, and Lloyds. These banks have started to offer Islamic financial products in some Arab countries, notably Bahrain and the United Arab Emirates, and to a lesser extent in the Western world where HSBC offers Islamic financial products such as home financing. A number of financial products also involve the acquisition of assets (i.e., real estate and small companies) in the West in "Islamically-structured" financing deals.[9]

Beginning with the Quran, Islamic tradition has always had concerns about economic transactions in relation to social and economic justice.[10] One issue which the Quran indirectly addresses is that of considering money as a "product" rather than a means of exchange. In other words, the Quran regards money as a measure of goods and services, and not itself a basis for making more money.[11] Today's high-frequency world of global transactions is built on the approach that one can make money by loaning or investing it without producing anything, in a never-ending reliance on debt.

The majority of Muslims have managed quite well by simply going along with the established Westernized banking and market systems. However, there is an increasing market interest in devising creative strategies to make money work according to the principle that all parties to financial transactions (not only the lender) must share equally in the risk as well as the profits.[12] In other words, Islamic finance is based on the concept of profit-loss sharing (PLS) where the focus of *all* parties involved is on the long-term success of the venture being funded, rather than on a quick return on investment. Furthermore, Muslim investors are required to screen their options carefully as the end criterion isn't the promise of highest returns, but the certainty that the eventual product or service will be compatible with underlying Islamic values (i.e., no stocks in companies that produce alcohol, pork, weapons, or pornography, or that offer gaming).[13] In a similar approach, Islamic banking provides for interest-free loans to the most needy.

The Quran forbids *riba*, a term generally understood to mean "taking interest" or "usury." However, Muslim scholars and economists don't always agree on what that precisely means in today's complex capital markets. As such, Muslims involved in implementing traditional Islamic values in the global financial arena face a big challenge; but despite differing opinions, the underlying objective is to ensure social equity—that is, to keep the urge for profit-making subordinate to higher principles. This is probably Islam's biggest contribution to business ethics in our time.[14] Much less antagonistic than the financial dealings common in the West, the emphasis of Islamic finance is on cooperation so that the client is primarily a partner.

In practice, developments in Islamic finance have been mostly limited to the field of lending. As indicated, the first modern Islamic bank was established in the 1970s, but over the past four decades the offering has grown significantly.[15] Plush magazines targeting Muslims now include numerous ads for businesses that solicit participation from people looking for prudent investment opportunities in stocks, bonds, and real estate that are also religiously acceptable (halal).

The recent financial meltdown in the West, which was caused by the excessive use of debt in the real estate sector, lax underwriting standards, and greed didn't impact Muslim countries as much, because they applied prudent lending terms, especially in Egypt and Saudi Arabia. For example, Egypt's financial system has one of the world's lowest loans-to-deposits ratios at 57 percent (the ratio in the US is a whopping 358 percent),[16] while Egyptian banks are not allowed to lend more than 5 percent of their capital to real estate,[17] which can be a high-risk sector when excessive debt floods the market. In addition, most Egyptians buy their homes with cash, as they are aware of the Islamic teachings associated with riba. This indicates that the prudent application of certain teachings from sharia law does have benefits in today's fast-moving financial markets.

## SHARIA

Sharia is an Arabic word that means "the way" or "the path." Sharia law is based on acquired knowledge that's derived from the teachings of the Quran, the sunna (the practices of the Prophet Muhammad), and *fatwas*—the rulings of Islamic scholars.

It's important to note that sharia was not in existence during the life of the Prophet, and that it reflected the sociopolitical realities of the period during which it was formalized. Originally an agrarian law code, it was designed by learned, male Muslim jurists during the Abbasid Caliphate (750–1258) to regulate all aspects of life in Muslim societies, from the behavior and habits of individuals to the workings of the criminal justice system and commerce. Sharia was, and still is, used to refer to both an Islamic system of law and the totality of an Islamic way of life. It is a religious code for living that's comparable to the Jewish Halakhah.

The rulings of sharia law have been divided by Muslim jurists into five categories or degrees of approval: obligatory (*wajib/fard*), recommended (*mustahab*), religiously indifferent or neutral (*mubah*), reprehensible (*makruh*), and prohibited (*haraam*).[18]

The rulings that are categorized as religiously indifferent (which must also be legally valid) are quite flexible, can be restructured in a modern context, and are open to reinterpretation and reform by Muslim jurists. This flexible category of rulings pertains to such issues as human rights, secularization, and Islamic finance. The other four categories—obligatory, recommended, reprehensible, and prohibited—are comprised of rigid religious rulings, the discussion of which is beyond the scope of this book.

Sharia is adopted by most Muslims to a greater or lesser degree as a matter of personal conscience, but it can also be formally instituted as law by certain states and enforced by the courts. Several Islamic countries have adopted some elements of sharia law, primarily in the areas of inheritance, banking, and contract law, while others adopt a hybrid of sharia and Western legal doctrines. Of the fifty-seven Muslim states that make up the membership of the Organization of the Islamic Conference (OIC)[19], only six countries—Pakistan, Iran, Saudi Arabia, Egypt, Sudan, and Nigeria—have adopted various aspects of sharia law in their constitutions, with Saudi Arabia being the strictest.

### PROTECTING MUSLIM SOCIETIES FROM THEFT

Islamic teachings in the Quran are there for the long-term benefit of Muslims, not their detriment. Sharia law has numerous virtues, but it also has specific rulings that have to be carefully understood by the West, namely the cutting off of hands for theft, and lashing for adultery. In accordance with the Quran, theft shall be punished by the amputation of hands:

*As for the man who steals*
*and the woman who steals,*
*cut off the hands for both of them*
*as a reward for what they have earned,*
*as an example from God.*
*And God is most powerful,*
*most judicious.*
*But God is relenting toward anyone*
*who repents and makes amends*
*after having done wrong;*
*for God is most forgiving,*
*most merciful.*[20]

However, before such a punishment is implemented, specific sharia-compliant criteria must be met, such as two eyewitnesses under oath saying that they actually saw the person stealing. If these witnesses cannot be produced, then the punishment cannot be carried out. It is also important to know that several additional requirements are in place pertaining to the amputation of hands, so its actual occurrence is extremely rare. These requirements are as follows: there must have been criminal intent to take private (not common) property; the theft must not have been the product of hunger, necessity, or duress; and the goods stolen must be over a minimum value, not prohibited (haraam), and not owned by the thief's family.[21]

All of these requirements must also be met under the scrutiny of judicial authority. While I completely understand why Westerners view this practice as being "barbaric," it can be quite effective in preventing theft in a Muslim society. For example, in Saudi Arabia (the only country that applies this punishment today), shop owners are able to leave their stores open while attending the five daily prayers in nearby mosques, because people in that society know the harsh punishment for stealing, which Islam clearly takes seriously. It takes only one such punishment to be seen in public to instill deep fear for many years in anyone who's contemplating theft.

### PROTECTING MUSLIM FAMILIES FROM ADULTERY

*"And do not approach adultery, for it is an obscenity and an evil way."* [22] In accordance with the Quran, lashing is the penalty for men and women who commit adultery. Similar to theft, there are several specific conditions related to those who commit it that must be met. One of the highly unlikely ones is that the punishment cannot be enforced unless there is a confession of the adulterer or adulteress, *or* four eyewitnesses who each saw the act actually being committed. All of these conditions also have to be met under the scrutiny of judicial authority. For men and women, the punishment prescribed in the Quran for adultery is one hundred lashes:

*The adulterer and the adulteress*
*are each to be whipped a hundred strokes;*
*and don't let compassion for them overcome you*
*where it concerns obedience to God…*
*And let a group of believers witness their punishment…*
*As for those who accuse*
*chaste women,*
*but fail to produce four witnesses,*
*whip them eighty strokes*

*and never take testimony*
*from them ever,*
*for they are the ones*
*who are immoral,*
*except those who repent after that*
*and make amends;*
*for God is most forgiving;*
*most merciful.*[23]

Again, this punishment may seem primitive to Westerners, but the long-term results can be effective in some Muslim societies. Adultery almost always leads to divorce and the destruction of families and their children's outlook on life. So if it can be prevented through harsh reprimand, then Muslim societies can benefit. At any rate, this retribution is carried out today only on extremely rare occasions in Afghanistan, Saudi Arabia, and Nigeria, which comprise a mere 7 percent of all the Muslim countries in the world.

## THE ILLEGITIMATE PRACTICE OF
## STONING TO DEATH

I would like to take the opportunity to discuss the issue of stoning people to death for adultery. Stoning has been used throughout history, in the form of community justice and as a judicial form of capital punishment. The practice is referred to in the Jewish texts of antiquity, but has long been abolished.

This bizarre practice is *not* mentioned anywhere in the Quran, and there are no strong hadith that support it. The most common Muslim view is that since the topic of stoning is not in the Quran, the practice is, therefore, null and goes against the existing verses related to this issue. Stoning most likely came from ancient practices during al-Jahiliyya that were incorrectly meshed into Islamic teachings. To that end, it should be widely condemned by all Muslims, and abolished.

Outside of a few million fanatics (out of the 1.57 billion Muslims worldwide), it can be argued that not many Muslims want the full establishment of sharia law in their countries, including those where sharia is already in place. Islam is a spiritual religion and a moral conduit through which Muslims can have a one-on-one relationship with God, without the intermediation of centralized and constitutional laws, or religious clerics. Accordingly, it is probably sufficient for Muslims to fully respect, understand, and apply the basic moral teachings of sharia in their daily lives without its incorporation as the rule of law at a national level. Therefore, sharia should be applied as guidance in matters of rituals, worship, and spirituality—a moral point of reference for Muslims, but not a constitutional *corpus*. That is because once Islam becomes entangled with state law, it becomes dangerously politicized, drifting away from its true essence and purpose.

### ISLAM AND DEMOCRACY

Islam is not a political ideology. Rather, Islam is a universal faith that emphasizes social justice and strongly denounces oppression. It has, most unfortunately, been politicized, misrepresented, and manipulated by extremists who have nothing to do with the essential teachings of the Prophet Muhammad and the Quran.

It should be noted that the lack of democracy in the majority of Muslim states does not suggest that democracy is not heralded by Islam *itself*, and having a dictatorship in a Muslim country certainly does not mean that it embraces the true spirit of Islam. By and large, it is an accident that most Muslim countries today are undemocratic in the Western sense, although it is hoped that this will gradually change with the recent "Arab Spring" revolutions. People in Muslim countries desperately want to be ruled by democracy, not by the oppressive and regressive regimes which came to power in the post-colonial period that started in the 1950s and 1960s. Muslims also desire a higher standard of living, so it is natural for them to want what the West has—things such as better health care, better housing, the freedom of expression, and access to information. But, sadly, many Muslims have been subjects of dictatorships and an ultra-conservative religious class, discouraging the exercise of inquiry which gave rise to the West's higher standard of living.

Consultation, which is a pillar of democracy, is an obligatory principle in Islam[24] which few Muslim governments actually adhere to today. When the Prophet Muhammad was not inspired by divine guidance in a specific issue or problem, he consulted his companions and acted according to the opinion of the majority, even if it was contrary to his own opinion.[25] An example of this was his consultation (*shura*) concerning the Battle of Uhud in 625. Muhammad was of the opinion that the Muslims shouldn't set out to fight, yet he submitted to the opinion of the majority who advocated fighting, and the result was defeat. Despite this, the Quran emphasized the necessity of consultation and addressed the Prophet in the following verse:

*So pardon them and seek forgiveness for them;*
*and consult with them in matters of concern.*
*Then when you have made a decision,*
*put your trust in God.*[26]

Islam has left to the judgment of Muslims the appropriate method of consultation that should benefit the interests of their communities.[27] In other words, if the welfare of a Muslim nation requires that consultation should follow the system practiced by more modern and advanced nations, Islam would not object to that system. Islam preaches that the application of judgment via consultation must also take into account the prevalent circumstances of every era.[28]

Furthermore, Islam permits people to have different opinions and allows interpretative judgment in religious matters, provided that these individuals fulfill the necessary qualifications to do so. Muslim scholars of the doctrines of jurisprudence (*al-Fuqahaa*) have come across many different opinions concerning several matters over the centuries, yet none have claimed that a difference of opinion is prohibited by Islam. Accordingly, the Muslim faith allows the expression of differing opinions by different people without any limitations, provided that they are genuinely concerned with the welfare and security of their communities.[29]

## URGENT REFORM BY MUSLIMS

Muhammad Abdou (d. 1905), the grand mufti of Egypt, once said, "When I went to the West, I saw Islam but no Muslims; when I returned to the East, I saw Muslims but no Islam." What Abdou said in the late nineteenth century still holds true today.

Ironically, Islam and modernity are probably more compatible in the West where freedom of religion and the separation of religion and state make it easier. It is only those countries which enjoy separation of religion and state that seem to be socially and economically successful by Western standards. For the theocratic and oppressive Middle East and most of the rest of the Islamic world, such compatibility is a great challenge—but not impossible.

The Prophet Muhammad is known to have said that the essence of religion is to deal with people properly (*al-deen al-muaamala*). What the Prophet said is a million miles away from the way many Muslims are treating each other today. What strikes me the most in Muslim countries is the absence of basic Islamic principles that are intended to be practiced in daily life, such as fairness, honesty, respect, and mutual trust.

In Judaism there's an old saying: "Don't judge Judaism by the Jews." Perhaps the same could be said about Islam today. It breaks my heart to see that the majority of Muslims are in a crisis today, and that Islam is in a lengthy down-cycle that has been taking shape since the thirteenth century with the demise of the Islamic Caliphate.

Reform in certain aspects of Islamic theology and jurisprudence—as well as reinterpretations of popular notions of Islam that are consistent with (and supportive of) the tenets of modern life—are urgently needed. So what can Muslims do to reform the interpretation of their religion while still maintaining the true spirit of Islam? Although not without their costs, risks, and trade-offs, the following are my humble suggestions as to how a society can be both Islamic *and* adopt the general criteria of Western modernity:

♦ Instill personal determination to practice basic Islamic principles in daily life.

♦ Work on assimilation, less isolation, and community cohesion in the West.

♦ Publicly condemn any group or person calling for an act of violence in the name of Islam.[30]

♦ Bring back the vibrant spirit of reform (*islah*), revival (*tajdid*), and independent thinking (*ijtihad*) that thrived during the Islamic Caliphate.

♦ Build a knowledge-based society. Knowledge itself is crucial to the functioning of an open society, and is intimately linked to human development, freedom, justice, and dignity.

♦ Separate religion and politics. The law of the twenty-first-century state should be based on secular principles; the affairs of religion should be left to the clerics, and the affairs of the state to the politicians.

♦ Increase the rights of women, as they constitute more than half the population of the Muslim world.

♦ Discourage the female burqa (niqab) because it has nothing to do with Islam, has no benefits for Muslim communities, erases the identity of women, and has become a global symbol of backwardness.

## CONCLUSION

For many in the West, Islam is a medieval theology ill-suited for modern times. Since 9/11, numerous Western politicians have claimed that Muslims hate "our democracy and success." That is not true. Islam is a simple, rational, and practical religion; it is a faith that offers all the necessary tools for success in life, and the Quran assures Muslims that if their society is just, egalitarian, and knowledge-seeking, it shall prosper.

Moreover, true Islam is compatible with the best practices of Western modernity because it is a universal religion for all times, and times change. The faith of Islam—which is still relatively young compared to Judaism and Christianity—is still evolving, and the fact that most Muslim countries have not yet found an ideal polity for the twenty-first century does not mean that Islam *itself* is incompatible with Western modernity. It means that Muslims have to first instill reform and change in themselves and in their modus vivendi, then strive to adopt the best practices of Western modernity that are in unison with Islamic values. However, the need for change and reform is also required of the West itself. That is, the fight against Islamophobia will only be engaged when the West recognizes that all the followers of Abraham are part of a common Judeo-Christian-Islamic history and tradition.[31]

If the correct and sincere application of Islam at the personal level occurs, coupled with reform at the institutional level, then the Muslim faith will gradually be able to take on a shape that's compatible with Western modernity. This is already happening in varying degrees in such countries as Tunisia, Egypt, Libya, Turkey, Indonesia, and Malaysia. Even ultra-conservative Saudi Arabia is starting to take small steps toward increased women's rights, a strong focus on higher education, and participatory government under the leadership of King Abdullah.

Positive change that will enable Muslims to find their deserved space in Western modernity is bound to occur, especially after the recent and ongoing revolutions in the Middle East. But such change will only materialize if it is first accompanied by a personal determination to practice basic Islamic principles in daily life—a genuine will for transformation that emanates from within:

> *God does not change the condition of a people*
> *until they change their own condition.*
> *…and they have no protection besides God.*[32]

# Epilogue

Ever since its beginning, Islam has been engaged in a never-ending struggle against attempts to obliterate the universal beliefs for which it stands. There is no doubt that this will continue, but through better communication and shared knowledge, this struggle can take on a new form.

We all have an innate need to search for causes, and that is why I have attempted to explain the reasons behind the myths about Islam. The nine myths that I have ventured to undermine and debunk have calcified over the centuries, culminating into the pervasive misjudgment that the West is "the enemy of Islam."

The Muslim faith should not be viewed as the enemy of the West. Although not as "monastic" as, say, Buddhism or Confucianism, Islam is a deeply spiritual religion that promotes peace and serenity:

> *When the Quran is recited,*
> *listen to it silently,*
> *that you may experience mercy.*
> *And remember your Lord*
> *within your soul, humbly and meekly.*[1]

Similar to Judaism and Christianity, Islam has been incorrectly applied and misinterpreted by a few ignorant extremists. I believe that 90 percent of the hearts and minds of the 1.57 billion Muslims around the world are deeply distraught when such terrible events as 9/11—or the mindless rampage by a deranged Muslim that killed thirteen US soldiers in Fort Hood, Texas, in November 2009—happen.

Moderate Muslims recognize that militant extremists are the *real* enemies of Islam, and they desperately want to connect with the Western world and share in their grief—as they loathe violence and extremism, similar to the vast majority of Jews and Christians. In this roller-coaster world, we must, therefore, stand up together against the extremists.

To a large extent, the misunderstandings between the three divine religions are based on the distorted thinking that one faith is "superior" to the other. These misconceptions are also based on the self-absorbed attitude that extremist Jews, Christians, and Muslims tend to have: that "it is us—and not you—who are God's chosen people." The three monotheistic religions were never intended to clash in some kind of competition in which one group is supposed to defeat the other, or in which one group is "God's chosen people" and the other is not. Such attitudes are so preposterous that sometimes I wonder if this way of thinking is the reason why people leave organized religion altogether. We need to transcend the childish "us-versus-them" mentality and realize—once and for all—that there are good people and bad people in every tribe, nation, and religion.

Alarmists claim that Islam is overrunning the West. But is it Islam per se, or is it the tide of atheism combined with an underlying fear and rejection of organized religion that is also behind this claim? For example, religion in Britain has suffered a significant decline since the 1970s, and all indicators show a continued shift in British society in line with other European countries, such as France and the Netherlands. A survey conducted in the United Kingdom in 2005 indicated that only 31 percent of the population attends church on Sunday, a sharp decline from the 71 percent that was tracked in 1970.[2] According to the Barna Research Group in the US, only 47 percent of American adults attend church services on Sunday.[3] In response to these trends, political scientist Ronald Inglehart of the University of Michigan-Ann Arbor corroborates that, "Although church attendance is declining in nearly all advanced industrial societies, spiritual concerns more broadly defined are not. In fact, in most industrial societies, a growing share of the population is spending time thinking about the meaning and purpose of life."[4] In other words, spiritual hunger in the age of materialism is on the rise.

Religion and the maintaining of faith in God is a "skill" that requires discipline, many sacrifices, and hard work. Practicing religion doesn't come easily, especially in this fast-paced age of gadgets and endless distractions. But religion can help people answer the intricate questions about the meaning and purpose of life, although that can be only attained through the correct application and understanding of the original teachings of the three divine faiths. Regrettably, it's when moderate Jews, Christians, and Muslims see how a few extremists can hijack their faiths that they get turned off by the whole idea of organized religion, which also instigates the virus-like spreading of myths about one another.

As I've attempted to highlight in this book, the current prejudice against Islam is not *only* a result of the West's lack of understanding toward this religion, but is due to the fact that radical and militant Muslims have strayed from the true essence of Islam in such a way that fans the fires of hatred from the West, resulting in the widespread myths about its universal teachings and history. Unfortunately, it's difficult to point out a group of Muslims that's a model for true Islam today, as their social fabric has lost many of the basic values it had in the past, such as honesty, integrity, and a "live conscience." But there is always hope that this sad situation shall someday change.

Islam should be based on an intimate relationship with God and His scripture that translates into constant self-improvement and multiple benefits for society. For the Muslim faith to flourish, the destructive ideologies of made-up Islam and its dysfunctional leadership must be sidelined; otherwise, it will lengthen its current down-cycle and become more alienated from the West and, above all, from the original teachings of the Prophet Muhammad.

Extremist Muslim leaders have to break free of sloganeering and attempting to establish a utopian Islamic state, or a cross-border community of Muslims (the umma). Instead, they should get on with promoting effective governing, improving the education systems in their countries, and focusing on providing employment opportunities for their youthful masses.

An ideal Islamic society includes free speech, freedom from corruption and oppression, and social justice, all of which are still lacking in the majority of Muslim countries today. In other words, the naïve and impractical idea of establishing an umma should be permanently shelved because the world we live in today is so different from how it was some 1,400 years ago when Muhammad was the ultimate, irreplaceable leader of Islam.

Islam is a virtuous way of life that wasn't originally intended to be a political system, especially one that's based on oppression and harsh dogma. Muslim countries such as Turkey and Indonesia (that have sensibly separated state from religion) are faring relatively well both economically and politically, because they have embraced the realities of our modern era. On the other hand, countries such as Iran, Pakistan, and Saudi Arabia (which don't separate Islam from the state) have immense sociopolitical problems that breed extremism, which, in turn, contributes to the myths about Islam.

Time is running out, and the river of misunderstanding is rapidly flowing against the followers of the Muslim faith. Muslims must become much more involved in effective advocacy against extremism and anti-Islamic ignorance, so that they are viewed more favorably in the West, and to help to move away the fog of myths and the yoke of misunderstandings. In turn, the Judeo-Christian worldview must be more open to an unbiased investigation of Islam, searching out the facts about the history, theology, and philosophy of this global religion. In the words of the British author Karen Armstrong, "We have to tear down the centuries-old demonic images that we have of each other, rinse our minds from religious prejudice, and live a life of empathy each and every day."[5]

Despite rogue waves of anti-Islam hysteria, there could be a hopeful era of understanding emerging in the United States. According to a survey conducted by the Pew Forum on Religion & Public Life, the percentage of Americans who believe that Islam encourages violence has declined in recent years, while basic knowledge about the faith has shown promising increases.[6] Most Americans also believe Muslims are discriminated against, a finding that suggests empathy for a community that has been egged on by the Islamophobes of the "they-hate-us-for-our-freedoms" industry.

The writing of this book has in many ways been a conveyance of my personal journey through Islam. As a Muslim who has spent most of his life in the West, I confess that up to my late twenties I actually believed in the nine myths about Islam that I've attempted to debunk in this book. That's because I read literature about Islam that was written by biased Western observers, didn't read the Quran properly, and didn't see the misunderstandings between Jews, Christians, and Muslims that are based on centuries of inherited ignorance. Of course I was aware that Arabs and Muslims were portrayed negatively as intolerant fanatics in the Western media, and that there was emotional "baggage" between Jews and Muslims because of the Israeli-Palestinian conflict. But it wasn't until after the calamitous events of 9/11 that I woke up and became fully aware of the deep-rooted misconceptions and the unwarranted anxieties that exist between the West and Islam.

The primary aim of this book has been to break down the preconceptions of Islam. This book has also strived to clarify that Islam today should not be judged by the behavior of a few Muslims, to bridge the gap in understanding between the West and Muslims, and to portray the myths and realities about the religion in an objective manner—to transmit that the widespread prejudice against this universal faith must be unveiled, discussed openly, and eventually dissolved. Our acquired hatred that stems from our tribal instincts and ignorance about other religions and cultures serves no purpose other than to diminish the potential to improve the physical experience we are going through as spiritual beings in the brief time we are given in this world.

As we reach the end of this book, I would like to leave the reader with the Farewell Sermon of the Prophet Muhammad, which he gave to his followers on Mount Arafat during his pilgrimage to Mecca in 631, one year before his death.[7] It reflects his deep respect toward the female gender and frames his revolutionary message that preached social equality, tolerance, and justice for all humanity fourteen centuries ago. Muhammad's words remind us how far the collective body of Islam has gone astray from his teachings, and how deeply misunderstood Islam is today.

Yet at the same time, the Prophet's Farewell Sermon leaves us with a glint of hope that if the Muslim religion is applied as he had intended, then the myths about this universal faith may someday go away, allowing for the true essence of Islam to be brought to light once again.

"O People, lend me an attentive ear, for I know not whether after this year I shall ever be amongst you again. Therefore, listen to what I am saying to you carefully, and take these words to those who could not be present here today.

"O People, just as you regard this day, this city, as sacred, regard the life and property of every Muslim as a sacred trust. Return the goods entrusted to you to their rightful owners. Hurt no one so that no one may hurt you. Remember that you will indeed meet your Lord, and that He will indeed reckon your deeds. God has forbidden that you take usury [interest]; therefore, all interest obligations shall henceforth be waived. Your capital, however, is yours to keep and you shall not inflict nor suffer any inequity.

"Beware of Satan for the safety of your religion. He has lost all hope that he will ever be able to lead you astray in big things, so beware of following him in the small things in life.

"O men, it is true that you have certain rights with regard to your women, but they also have rights over you. Remember that you have taken them as your wives only under God's trust and with His permission. If they abide by your right, then to them belongs the right to be fed and clothed in kindness. Do treat your women well and be kind to them, for they are your committed partners.

"O People, listen to me in earnest, worship God, complete your five daily prayers, fast during the month of Ramadan, and give your wealth in charity. Perform the pilgrimage once in your lifetime, but only if you can afford to.

"All humankind is from one source. An Arab has no superiority over a non-Arab, nor a non-Arab has any superiority over an Arab; also a white has no superiority over a black, nor does a black have any superiority over a white, except by piety and good action. Learn that every Muslim is a brother and sister to every Muslim and that the Muslims constitute one united spirit. Nothing shall be legitimate to a Muslim which belongs to a fellow Muslim, unless it was given freely and willingly. Do not, therefore, do injustice to yourselves.

"Remember, one day you will appear before God and answer for your deeds. So beware, do not stray from the straight path of righteousness after I am gone.

"O People, no prophet or apostle will ever come after me, and no new faith will be born. Reason well, therefore, O People, and understand the words which I convey to you. I leave behind me two things: the Quran and my example of living through my humble way of life—so if you follow these, you shall never go astray.

"All those who listen to me shall pass on my words to others and those to others again; and may the last ones understand my words better than those who listen to me directly today.

"Be my witness, O Lord, that I have now completed my mission and have conveyed Your message to all of humanity."

# Acknowledgments

This book has been an enlightening journey that has taken three informative years to research and over two years to write. Writing in the early hours of the morning and during the calm of the night—with the reader always in mind—has been one of the greatest joys of my life.

This book would not have been possible without the unsparing assistance of Dr. Salem abd el-Gelil, Deputy Minister of Religious Endowments for Preaching in Egypt. The generous Dr. abd el-Gelil shared his vast knowledge about Islam and guided me to the most accurate sources.

My sincere gratitude goes to Dr. John L. Dodson, a United Methodist Church pastor who has served many congregations in Alaska, California, and Nevada. Dr. Dodson was most giving for reviewing the draft manuscript and providing his objective insight from the Christian perspective.

My thanks go to Dr. Naomi Seidman, Director of the Richard S. Dinner Center for Jewish Studies at the Graduate

Theological Union (GTU) in Berkeley, California, for her input on parts of the chapter related to Judaism.

My wife, Jasmine, was patient with my long hours, giving me a quiet space to write, bringing me coffee when I needed a break, and reading over the early manuscript to make sure it was enjoyable. I am so grateful for her love and support.

I would like to acknowledge my brother Hamdi for his rigorous critique of every word I wrote, as well as my mother, Marianne, and Dr. Robert Nebus for teaching me how to write in English. My father, a scholar with over twenty-five years of academic research experience, was also invaluable with his knowing comments. Lastly, my appreciation goes to Ahmad, Anthony, Ghada, Josephine, and Rayhaab for their unfailing support.

If this book is capable of changing the opinion of just one person who has misconceptions and misunderstandings about Islam, then I shall have fulfilled my humble goal.

# Appendix A

### The Ninety-nine Names of God

*The most beautiful names pertain to God.* (Quran: 20:8)

The ninety-nine names of God are His attributes that are mentioned in the Quran. In their aggregate, the names culminate into describing God as "Everything"—as "Being." It's not possible to perfectly translate the attributes from their original Arabic into English; however, the following are some fairly close explanations:

| # | Name In Arabic | Translation |
|---|---|---|
| 1. | Al-Rahman | The Most Merciful, Compassionate |
| 2. | Al-Rahim | The Most Merciful |
| 3. | Al-Malik | The Owner of Everything |
| 4. | Al-Qudduss | The Most Holy, Most Pure |
| 5. | Al-Salaam | The Peace and Blessing |
| 6. | Al-Mouemin | The Guarantor, Self-affirming |
| 7. | Al-Muhaymin | The Guardian, Preserver |
| 8. | Al-Aziz | The Almighty, Self-sufficient |
| 9. | Al-Jabbar | The Most Powerful, Irresistible |
| 10. | Al-Mutakabbir | The Tremendous |
| 11. | Al-Khaliq | The Creator |
| 12. | Al-Barie | The Rightful |
| 13. | Al-Musawwir | The Fashioner of Forms |
| 14. | Al-Ghaffar | The Ever-forgiving |
| 15. | Al-Qahhar | The All-compelling Subduer |
| 16. | Al-Wahhab | The Bestower |
| 17. | Al-Razzaq | The Ever-providing |
| 18. | Al-Fattah | The Opener, Victory Giver |
| 19. | Al-Aleem | The All-knowing, Omniscient |
| 20. | Al-Qabid | The Restrainer |
| 21. | Al-Bassit | The Expander, Munificent |
| 22. | Al-Khafid | The Abaser |
| 23. | Al-Rafea | The Exalter |
| 24. | Al-Muezz | The Giver of Honor |
| 25. | Al-Muzill | The Giver of Dishonor |
| 26. | Al-Samea | The All-hearing |
| 27. | Al-Basir | The All-seeing |
| 28. | Al-Hakam | The Judge, Arbitrator |
| 29. | Al-Adl | The Utterly Just |
| 30. | Al-Latif | The Gentle, Kind |
| 31. | Al-Khabir | The All-aware |
| 32. | Al-Halim | The Forbearing, Indulgent |

| 33. | *Al-Azim* | The Magnificent, Infinite |
|---|---|---|
| 34. | *Al-Ghafur* | The All-forgiving |
| 35. | *Al-Shakur* | The Thankful |
| 36. | *Al-Aliyy* | The Sublimely Exalted |
| 37. | *Al-Kabir* | The Great |
| 38. | *Al-Hafiz* | The Preserver, Protector |
| 39. | *Al-Muqeet* | The Nourisher |
| 40. | *Al-Hasib* | The Bringer of Judgment |
| 41. | *Al-Jalil* | The Majestic |
| 42. | *Al-Karim* | The Bountiful, Generous |
| 43. | *Al-Raqib* | The Watchful |
| 44. | *Al-Mujib* | The Responsive, Answerer |
| 45. | *Al-Wasea* | The Vast, All-encompassing |
| 46. | *Al-Hakim* | The Wise |
| 47. | *Al-Wadud* | The One Who Loves and Is Loved |
| 48. | *Al-Majid* | The All-glorious |
| 49. | *Al-Baaith* | The Raiser of the Dead |
| 50. | *Al-Shahid* | The Witness |
| 51. | *Al-Haqq* | The Truth |
| 52. | *Al-Wakil* | The Trustee, Dependable |
| 53. | *Al-Qawwiyy* | The Strong |
| 54. | *Al-Matin* | The Firm, Steadfast |
| 55. | *Al-Waliyy* | The Protecting Friend, Patron |
| 56. | *Al-Hamid* | The All-praiseworthy |
| 57. | *Al-Muhsi* | The Accounter, Numberer of All |
| 58. | *Al-Mubdi* | The Originator, Initiator of Everything |
| 59. | *Al-Muid* | The Restorer |
| 60. | *Al-Muhyi* | The Giver of Life |
| 61. | *Al-Mumit* | The Bringer of Death |
| 62. | *Al-Hayy* | The Ever-living |
| 63. | *Al-Qayyum* | The Self-subsisting Provider |
| 64. | *Al-Wajid* | The Perceiver, Finder |
| 65. | *Al-Majid* | The Illustrious, Magnificent |

| 66. | Al-Wahid | The One, Unique |
|---|---|---|
| 67. | Al-Ahad | The One, All-inclusive, Indivisible |
| 68. | Al-Samad | The Self-sufficient |
| 69. | Al-Qadir | The All-able |
| 70. | Al-Muqtadir | The All-determiner, Dominant |
| 71. | Al-Muqaddim | The Expediter, He Who Brings Forward |
| 72. | Al-Muakhir | The Delayer, He Who Puts Far Away |
| 73. | Al-Awwal | The First (Alpha) |
| 74. | Al-Akhir | The Last (Omega) |
| 75. | Al-Zahir | The Manifest, All-victorious |
| 76. | Al-Batin | The Hidden, All-encompassing |
| 77. | Al-Wali | The Patron |
| 78. | Al-Mutaali | The Self-exalted |
| 79. | Al-Barr | The Most Kind and Righteous |
| 80. | Al-Tawwab | The Ever-returning, Ever-relenting |
| 81. | Al-Muntaqim | The Avenger |
| 82. | Al-Afuww | The Pardoner, Effacer of Sins |
| 83. | Al-Raouf | The Compassionate, All-pitying |
| 84. | Malik al-Mulk | The Owner of All Sovereignty |
| 85. | Zul Jalal wal-Ikram | The Lord of Majesty and Generosity |
| 86. | Al-Muqsit | The Equitable |
| 87. | Al-Jamea | The Gatherer, Unifier |
| 88. | Al-Ghaniyy | The All-rich, Independent |
| 89. | Al-Mughni | The Enricher, Emancipator |
| 90. | Al-Manea | The Withholder, Shielder, Defender |
| 91. | Al-Daar | The Distressor, Afflictor |
| 92. | Al-Nafea | The Benefactor |
| 93. | Al-Nur | The Light |
| 94. | Al-Hadi | The Guide |
| 95. | Al-Badeea | The Incomparable, Originator |
| 96. | Al-Baqi | The Ever-enduring, Immutable |
| 97. | Al-Warith | The Heir, Inheritor of All |
| 98. | Al-Rashid | The Guide, Infallible Teacher |
| 99. | Al-Sabur | The Patient, Timeless |

# Appendix B

## The 114 Chapters of the Quran

In the following table, the names of the Quran's 114 chapters appear in Arabic in their actual Quranic order, followed by their estimated chronological order of revelation, and then their English translation:[1]

| Quranic Order[2] | Chronological Order[3] | Transliteration in Arabic | Translation in English |
|---|---|---|---|
| 1. | 5 | *Al-Fatiha* | The Opening |
| 2. | 87 | *Al-Baqara* | The Cow |
| 3. | 89 | *Aal-Emraan* | The Family of Amran |
| 4. | 92 | *Al-Nisaa* | Women |
| 5. | 112 | *Al-Maida* | The Table |

| 6. | 55 | *Al-Anaam* | Cattle |
|---|---|---|---|
| 7. | 39 | *Al-Aaraaf* | The Heights |
| 8. | 88 | *Al-Anfal* | Spoils of War |
| 9. | 113 | *Al-Tawba* | Repentance |
| 10. | 51 | *Yunus* | Jonah |
| 11. | 52 | *Hud* | Hud |
| 12. | 53 | *Yusuf* | Joseph |
| 13. | 96 | *Al-Raad* | Thunder |
| 14. | 72 | *Ibrahim* | Abraham |
| 15. | 54 | *Al-Hijar* | The Stones |
| 16. | 70 | *Al-Nahl* | The Bees |
| 17. | 50 | *Al-Israa* | The Night Journey |
| 18. | 69 | *Al-Kahf* | The Cave |
| 19. | 44 | *Maryam* | Mary |
| 20. | 45 | *Ta-Ha* | Ta-Ha |
| 21. | 73 | *Al-Anbiyaa* | The Prophets |
| 22. | 103 | *Al-Hajj* | The Pilgrimage |
| 23. | 74 | *Al-Muminoun* | The Believers |
| 24. | 102 | *Al-Nour* | Light |
| 25. | 42 | *Al-Furqan* | The Criterion |
| 26. | 47 | *Al-Shuaraa* | The Poets |
| 27. | 48 | *Al-Naml* | The Ants |
| 28. | 49 | *Al-Qassas* | The Stories |
| 29. | 85 | *Al-Ankabout* | The Spider |
| 30. | 84 | *Al-Roum* | The Romans |
| 31. | 57 | *Luqman* | Luqman |
| 32. | 75 | *Al-Sajda* | Worship |
| 33. | 90 | *Al-Ahzab* | The Confederates |
| 34. | 58 | *Sabaa* | Sheba |
| 35. | 43 | *Faatir* | Creator |
| 36. | 41 | *Ya-Seen* | Ya-Seen |
| 37. | 56 | *Al-Saffaat* | Standing Together |
| 38. | 38 | *Saadd* | Saadd |

| | | | |
|---|---|---|---|
| 39. | 59 | *Al-Zummar* | The Crowds |
| 40. | 60 | *Ghafir* | The Believer |
| 41. | 61 | *Fussilatt* | Hah-Meem: Worship |
| 42. | 62 | *Al-Shura* | Consultation |
| 43. | 63 | *Al-Zukhruf* | Decoration |
| 44. | 64 | *Al-Dukhan* | Smoke |
| 45. | 65 | *Al-Gathiya* | Kneeling |
| 46. | 66 | *Al-Ahqaf* | The Winding Sands |
| 47. | 95 | *Muhammad* | Muhammad |
| 48. | 111 | *Al-Fateh* | Victory |
| 49. | 106 | *Al-Hujurat* | The Private Chambers |
| 50. | 34 | *Qaff* | Qaff: Worship |
| 51. | 67 | *Al-Dhariyat* | The Scattering Wind |
| 52. | 76 | *Al-Toor* | The Mountain |
| 53. | 23 | *Al-Nijm* | The Star |
| 54. | 37 | *Al-Qamar* | The Moon |
| 55. | 97 | *Al-Rahman* | The Most Merciful |
| 56. | 46 | *Al-Waqia* | The Inevitable |
| 57. | 94 | *Al-Hadeed* | Iron |
| 58. | 105 | *Al-Mujadila* | She Who Disputes |
| 59. | 101 | *Al-Hashr* | The Gathering |
| 60. | 91 | *Al-Mumtahana* | The Woman on Trial |
| 61. | 109 | *Al-Saff* | The Battle Line |
| 62. | 110 | *Al-Jumua* | The Congregation |
| 63. | 104 | *Al-Munafiqun* | The Hypocrites |
| 64. | 108 | *Al-Taghabun* | Outdoing |
| 65. | 99 | *Al-Talaaq* | Divorce |
| 66. | 107 | *Al-Tahreem* | Prohibition |
| 67. | 77 | *Al-Mulk* | Dominion |
| 68. | 2 | *Al-Qalam* | The Pen |
| 69. | 78 | *Al-Haaqqa* | The Momentous Event |
| 70. | 79 | *Al-Maarij* | The Ascending Steps |
| 71. | 71 | *Nuh* | Noah |

| 72. | 40 | *Al-Jinn* | The Sprites |
|---|---|---|---|
| 73. | 3 | *Al-Muzzammil* | Wrapping Himself |
| 74. | 4 | *Al-Muddathir* | Covering Himself |
| 75. | 31 | *Al-Qiyama* | The Resurrection |
| 76. | 98 | *Al-Insan* | The Human Being |
| 77. | 33 | *Al-Mursalat* | Those Sent Forth |
| 78. | 80 | *Al-Nabaa* | The Announcement |
| 79. | 81 | *Al-Naziaat* | The Snatchers |
| 80. | 24 | *Abasa* | He Frowned |
| 81. | 7 | *Al-Takwir* | The Rolling Up |
| 82. | 82 | *Al-Infitar* | The Splitting |
| 83. | 86 | *Al-Mutafifeen* | The Cheaters |
| 84. | 83 | *Al-Inshiqaaq* | Bursting Open |
| 85. | 27 | *Al-Burouj* | The Constellations |
| 86. | 36 | *Al-Tariq* | The Wayfarer |
| 87. | 8 | *Al-Aalaa* | The Highest |
| 88. | 68 | *Al-Ghashiya* | The Calamity |
| 89. | 10 | *Al-Fajr* | Dawn |
| 90. | 35 | *Al-Balad* | The City |
| 91. | 26 | *Al-Shams* | The Sun |
| 92. | 9 | *Al-Layl* | The Night |
| 93. | 11 | *Al-Duha* | The Morning |
| 94. | 12 | *Al-Sharh* | The Expansion |
| 95. | 28 | *Al-Tein* | The Fig |
| 96. | 1 | *Al-Alaq* | Read! |
| 97. | 25 | *Al-Qadar* | The Decree |
| 98. | 100 | *Al-Bayyina* | The Evidence |
| 99. | 93 | *Al-Zilzal* | The Earthquake |
| 100. | 14 | *Al-Adiyat* | The Chargers |
| 101. | 30 | *Al-Qaria* | The Day of Resurrection |
| 102. | 16 | *Al-Takathur* | Vying for More |
| 103. | 13 | *Al-Asr* | The Age |
| 104. | 32 | *Al-Humaza* | The Backbiter |

| 105. | 19 | *Al-Fil* | The Elephant |
|------|-----|-------------|------------------------|
| 106. | 29 | *Al-Quraysh* | Quraysh |
| 107. | 17 | *Al-Maoun* | Assistance |
| 108. | 15 | *Al-Kauthar* | Abundance |
| 109. | 18 | *Al-Kafiroun* | The Blasphemers |
| 110. | 114 | *Al-Nasr* | Victory |
| 111. | 6 | *Al-Lahab* | Flame |
| 112. | 22 | *Al-Ikhlas* | Pure Truth (Sincerity) |
| 113. | 20 | *Al-Falaq* | Dawn |
| 114. | 21 | *Al-Naas* | Humankind |

**NOTES:**

1.  T. Cleary, *The Quran: A New Translation,* (Burr Ridge, IL: Starlatch Press, 2004).

2.  As presented, the Quran is comprised of 114 chapters (suras). The "Quranic Order" indicated in the table above is based on the numerical order of the 114 chapters compiled by Othman ibn Affan, the third caliph of Islam. Muslims believe that Othman commissioned a committee to produce a standard copy of the text of the Quran, which was meticulously researched and compiled after the death of Muhammad in 632, and finalized some twenty years later. This Quranic Order is also believed to be based on specific instructions by the Prophet on how the Quran should be structured and never altered. Generally, the order of the 114 chapters is from the longest sura to the shortest. The 114 chapters are also structured in a logical order of relevance by subject and underlying message (i.e., chapters 91, 92, and 93 are about the sun, the night, and the morning, and so forth).

3.  The order of revelation of each of the chapters is based
    on the "best effort" research conducted by the Indian-
    Muslim scholar Abdullah Yusuf Ali (d. 1953). Studying
    the chronological order of the Quran is an excellent
    way to learn about the events surrounding the life of the
    Prophet Muhammad. It should be noted, however, that
    the chronological order is general, because several verses
    within some chapters are not sequential in terms of the
    timing of their revelation to the Prophet.

# Appendix C

**Translations of Chapter 3**

**("The Family of Amran")**
**and Chapter 19 ("Mary")**[1]

The following is the English translation of selected verses from "The Family of Amran"[2] and "Mary" chapters of the Quran. For brevity, I have included only those verses that are directly relevant to Jesus and Mary:

**SELECTED VERSES FROM CHAPTER 3, "THE FAMILY OF AMRAN":**

*33....God chose over all people*
   *Adam and Noah,*

*and the family of Abraham*
*and the family of Amran,*

34. *offspring one of the other.*
    *And God is all-hearing, all-knowing.*

35. *A woman of Amran said,*
    *"My Lord, I devote what is in my womb*
    *exclusively to the service of God;*
    *so accept this from me,*
    *for You are the all-hearing, the all-knowing."*

36. *Then when she gave birth to her,*
    *she said, "My Lord,*
    *I have given birth to a girl,"—*
    *though God knew better what she bore—*
    *"and the male is not like the female.*
    *And I have named her Mary;*
    *and I commend her*
    *and her progeny*
    *to Your protection*
    *from Satan the accursed."*

37. *Her Lord accepted her,*
    *with a gracious reception,*
    *and caused her to grow up beautifully,*
    *and entrusted her to Zacharias.*
    *Whenever Zacharias went to her*
    *in her private chamber,*
    *he found supplies with her.*
    *He said, "Mary, where do you get this?"*
    *She said, "It is from God;*
    *for God provides*
    *for whomever God will,*
    *beyond any accounting."*

38. *There Zacharias prayed to his Lord.*
    *He said, "My Lord, grant me*
    *good progeny from You;*
    *for You hear prayer."*

39. *Then the angels called him*
    *while he was standing there*
    *praying in the room,*
    *saying, "God gives you glad tidings of John,*
    *verifying a word from God, noble, chaste;*
    *a prophet, one of the righteous."*

40. *He said, "My Lord, how can I have a son,*
    *as I am already old, and my wife is barren?"*
    *Thus God does what God wills.*

41. *He said, "My Lord,*
    *give me a sign."*
    *"Your sign is that you shall not speak*
    *to anyone for three days,*
    *except by signals.*
    *And remember your Lord a lot,*
    *and glorify God*
    *in the evening and the morning."*

42. *And the angels said, "O Mary,*
    *God has chosen you and purified you,*
    *chosen you over the women of all peoples.*

43. *Mary, obey your Lord devoutly.*
    *Worship, and bow in prayer*
    *with those bowing with prayer."*

44. *That is from communications of the unseen,*
    *which We intimate to you.*
    *You were not with them*
    *when they were casting lots to decide*

*which of them would support Mary,*
*and you were not with them*
*when they were arguing.*

45. *The angels said,*
    *"O Mary, God gives you good news*
    *of a word from God,*
    *named the Messiah,*
    *Jesus Son of Mary,*
    *honored in the world and the hereafter,*
    *and one of the intimates of God.*

46. *And he will speak to the people*
    *in infancy and maturity,*
    *and be one of the righteous."*

47. *She said, "My Lord!*
    *How can I have a son,*
    *when no man has touched me?"*
    *Thus does God create at will:*
    *when God decides on something,*
    *God simply says to it "Be!"*
    *And it is...*

50. *"And verifying the Torah before me,*
    *and to legitimize for you*
    *some of what had been forbidden you,*
    *I have come to you with a sign*
    *from your Lord.*
    *So be conscious of God and obey me."*

51. *"It is God that is my Lord*
    *and your Lord, so serve God;*
    *this is a straight path."*

52. *Then when Jesus perceived*
    *atheism among them,*

*he said, "Who will be my allies*
*on the way to God?"*
*The disciples said, "We are allies of God.*
*We believe in God; witness*
*that we surrender to Him."*

53. *"Our Lord,*
*we believe in what You have revealed,*
*and we follow the emissary;*
*so record us among the witnesses."*

54. *Yet they plotted,*
*but God plotted too;*
*and God is the best of plotters.*

55. *God said, "Jesus,*
*I will take you unto Myself,*
*and I will elevate you to Me,*
*and clear you of those who scoff,*
*and place those who follow you*
*above those who scoff,*
*until the day of resurrection.*
*Then you all will return to Me,*
*and I will judge among you*
*on matters on which you disagree..."*

59. *Jesus was to God like Adam was:*
*God created him from dust,*
*then said, "Be!" and he was.*

60. *Truth is from your Lord,*
*So do not be a doubter...*

62. *This is the true story:*
*There is no God but God.*
*And God is the Mighty, the Wise.*

## Selected Verses from Chapter 19, "Mary":

*1. K.H.Y.A.S.*[3]

*2. A recitation of the mercy of your Lord*
*on the devotee Zacharias.*

*3. He called on his Lord*
*with a secret cry,*

*4. saying, "My Lord, my bones*
*have become feeble,*
*and my hair has turned white,*
*but I have never been disappointed*
*in praying to You.*

*5. Now I fear my relatives after me,*
*as my wife is barren.*
*So give me a son from You,*

*6. who will be my heir,*
*and succeed to the lineage of Jacob.*
*And, my Lord, make him acceptable."*

*7. **"O Zacharias: We bring you good news***
***of a son, whose name will be John (Yahya);***
***We have not attributed it***
***as a namesake before."***[4]

*8. He said, "My Lord,*
*how will I have a son*
*when my wife is barren*
*and I have become*
*decrepit with age?"*

*9. It will be so: your Lord says,*
***"That is easy for Me,***
***since I created you before,***
***when you had been nothing."***

10. *"My Lord, give me a sign."*
   **"Your sign shall be**
   **that you not speak to people**
   **for three nights in a row."**

11. *Then he came out*
   *from his prayer niche to his people*
   *and told them to praise God*
   *in the morning and the evening.*

12. **"John, hold strongly to scripture."**
   *And We gave him wisdom,*
   *even as a boy;*

13. *and compassion from Us,*
   *and innocence.*
   *And he was conscientious,*

14. *and kind to his parents;*
   *and he was not insolent or defiant.*

15. *So peace upon him*
   *the day he was born*
   *and the day he dies,*
   *and the day he will be*
   *resurrected, alive.*

16. *And mention Mary in the Book:*
   *when she withdrew from her people*
   *to a place in the east,*

17. *and secluded herself from them,*
   *We sent her Our spirit [an angel],*
   *which appeared to her like a man.*

18. *She said,*
   *"I take refuge from you*
   *with the Benevolent One,*
   *if you are conscientious."*

19. *He [the angel] said, "I am only*
    *a messenger from your Lord,*
    *to give you a sinless son."*

20. *She said, "How will I have a son,*
    *when no man has touched me*
    *and I have not been unchaste?"*

21. *He said, "It will be so."*
    *He said, "Your Lord says,*
    *'It is easy for Me; and We intend*
    *to make him a sign for humankind,*
    *and a mercy from Us.'*
    *So the matter is decided."*

22. *So she carried him [Jesus],*
    *secluding herself with him*
    *in a faraway place.*

23. *Then labor pains impelled her*
    *to the trunk of a palm tree.*
    *She said, "Would that I had*
    *died before this*
    *and been completely forgotten!"*

24. *Then he called to her from below,*
    *saying, "Do not grieve;*
    *your Lord has put a stream beneath you,*

25. *and shake the trunk of the palm toward you*
    *to let fresh ripe dates fall by you.*

26. *Then eat and drink and be of good cheer:*
    *but if you see any man, say, 'I have dedicated*
    *a fast to the Benevolent One, so I shall not*
    *talk to any human being today.'"*

27. *Finally she carried him*
    *to her people: they said, "Mary,*

you sure have done
an unheard-of thing!

28. O sister of Aaron,[5]
your father was not a bad man,
and your mother was not a whore."

29. Now she pointed at him.
They said, "How can we talk to one
who is an infant in the cradle?"

30. He said, "I am indeed the servant of God,
who has given me scripture
and made me a prophet,

31. and made me blessed wherever I am;
and has prescribed prayer and charity
for me as long as I live,

32. and kindness to my mother as well;
and did not make me an arrogant malcontent.

33. And peace is upon me
the day I was born,
and the day I die
and the day I am resurrected,
alive."

34. That was Jesus, Son of Mary,
a word of truth about which they doubt.

35. Having a son
is not attributable to God,
who is beyond that,
and when having determined something
merely says to it "Be!"
And it is.

## NOTES:

1. T. Cleary, The Quran: A New Translation, (Burr Ridge, IL: Starlatch Press, 2004).

2. Amran (*Emraan* in Arabic) is the name of the father of the Prophets Aaron and Moses. In Exodus 6:20, the name used is "Amram."

3. According to the Muslim scholar Abdullah Yusuf Ali, certain chapters in the Quran have specific initials prefixed to them, which are called the "abbreviated letters." A number of conjectures have been made as to their meaning. Opinions are divided as to the exact meaning of each particular letter, or combination of letters, but it is agreed that they have a mystical meaning that's beyond our comprehension. In this specific verse, the four mystical letters are "K.H.Y.A.S." (*Kaaf hih yeh aeen saad* in Arabic).

4. Change in font to emphasize the direct speaking of God.

5. In this verse, Mary is referred to as the "sister of Aaron." The Quran is not, of course, claiming that Mary was literally the sister of Aaron, the brother of Moses. Many Islamic scholars indicate that Mary had a brother named after the Prophet Aaron, which could have been possible as many gave their children names of apostles and pious persons. Abdullah Yusuf Ali says in his classic translation and commentary on the Quran, "Mary is reminded of her high lineage," meaning that she was a blood descendant of the Prophets Aaron and Moses, and she was, therefore, given a title of honor after a name of an apostle of whose lineage she came from.

# Appendix D

### Quotes about Islam and the
### Prophet Muhammad

The following quotations reflect the sentiment of several global leaders toward Islam:

"No religion condones the murder of innocent men, women, and children. But our actions were aimed at fanatics and killers who wrap murder in the cloak of righteousness, and in so doing, profane the great religion of Islam in whose name they act."

—*Bill Clinton, US President*
*August 20, 1998*

"We honor the universal values that are embodied in Islam—love of family and community, mutual respect, the power of education, and the deepest yearning of all: to live in peace. Values that can bring people of every faith and culture together, strengthen us as a people, and, I would argue, strengthen the United States as a nation."

*—Hillary Clinton, former First Lady and*
*US Senator; US Secretary of State*
*January 21, 1999*

"We are all human beings, and we all believe that we should do unto others as we would have done unto us. And I think the message is clear: Islam is a religion for peace."

*—Kofi Annan, UN Secretary-General*
*September 14, 2001*

"The doctrine and teachings of Islam are those of peace and harmony. I read the Quran—the God of the Quran is merciful and forgiving. It is a whole teaching dedicated to building peace in the world."

*—Tony Blair, British Prime Minister*
*September 19, 2001*

"There was once a civilization that was the greatest in the world. It was able to create a continental super-state that stretched from ocean to ocean and from northern climes to tropics and deserts. Within its dominion lived hundreds of millions of people, of different creeds and ethnic origins...One of its languages became the universal language of much of the world, the bridge between the peoples of a hundred lands. Its armies were made up of people of many nationalities, and its military protection allowed a degree of peace and prosperity that had never been known. The reach of this civilization's commerce extended from Latin America to China, and everywhere in between...And this civilization was driven more than anything by invention. Its architects designed buildings that defied gravity. Its mathematicians created the algebra and algorithms that would enable the building of computers, and the creation of encryption. Its doctors examined the human body, and found new cures for disease. Its astronomers looked into the heavens, named the stars, and paved the way for space travel and exploration...Its writers created thousands of stories—stories of courage, romance, and magic. Its poets wrote of love, when others before them were too steeped in fear to think of such things...When other nations were afraid of ideas, this civilization thrived on them, and kept them alive. When censors threatened to wipe out knowledge from past civilizations, this civilization kept the knowledge alive, and passed it on to others...While modern Western civilization shares many of these traits, the civilization I'm talking about was the Islamic world."

*—Carly Fiorina, CEO of Hewlett-Packard*
*September 26, 2001*


"But the really right answer is, 'What if he [Barack Obama] is?' Is there something wrong with being a Muslim in this country? The answer's no, that's not America. Is there something wrong with some seven-year-old Muslim-American kid believing that he or she could be president?"

*—Colin Powell, Chairman of Joint Chiefs of Staff of*
*the US Armed Forces and US Secretary of State*
*October 19, 2008*

"Let me say this as clearly as I can…the United States is not, and never will be, at war with Islam."

*—Barack Obama, US President*
*April 5, 2009*

᪥

In addition, the following quotations are examples of how the Prophet Muhammad and his religion have been revered by some of the world's leading intellectuals:

"I wanted to know the best of the life of one who holds today an undisputed sway over the hearts of millions of mankind…I became more than ever convinced that it was not the sword that won a place for Islam in those days in the scheme of life. It was the rigid simplicity, the utter self-effacement of the Prophet, the scrupulous regard for pledges, his intense devotion to his friends and followers, his intrepidity, his fearlessness, and his absolute trust in God and in his own mission. These, and not the sword, carried everything before them and surmounted every obstacle. When I closed the second volume [of the Prophet's biography], I was sorry there was not more for me to read of that great life."

*—Mahatma Gandhi's statement published in*
Young India (1924)

"The Muslim religion will prevail throughout the world as it is in conformity with both the mind and wisdom."

*—Leo Tolstoy in* The Things Which Humans
Should Know (1909)

**Note:** *The Things Which Humans Should Know* was Tolstoy's treatise about the Prophet Muhammad, which has been known among European publishers for more than one hundred years, but unknown to readers in the US. The book was originally published in Russia in 1909.

"My choice of Muhammad to lead the list of the world's most influential persons may surprise some readers and may be questioned by others, but he was the only man in history who was supremely successful on both the secular and religious level...It is probable that the relative influence of Muhammad on Islam has been larger than the combined influence of Jesus Christ and St. Paul on Christianity...It is this unparalleled combination of secular and religious influence which I feel entitles Muhammad to be considered the most influential single figure in human history."

*—Michael H. Hart in* The 100: A Ranking of the
Most Influential Persons In History (1998)

"No religion is more worldly than Islam."

*—V. S. Naipaul in* Among the Believers:
An Islamic Journey (1982)

"I believe that if a man like him [Muhammad] were to assume the leadership of the modern world, he would succeed in solving its problems in a way that would bring it the much needed peace and happiness: I have prophesied about the faith of Muhammad that it would be acceptable to the Europe of tomorrow as it is beginning to be acceptable to the Europe of today. Medieval ecclesiastics, either through ignorance or bigotry, painted Muhammadanism [Islam] in the darkest colors. They were, in fact, trained to hate both the man Muhammad and his religion. To them, Muhammad was an anti-Christ. I have studied him, the wonderful man, and in my opinion, far from being an anti-Christ, he must be called the Savior of Humanity."

—*Sir George Bernard Shaw in*
The Genuine Islam (1936)

# Appendix E

## Questions for Discussion

1.  What was your perception of Islam before reading *Prejudice Unveiled: The Myths and Realities about Islam,* and has it been changed or confirmed? In what ways, if any, has it changed?
2.  What perspective(s) in the book did you find surprising or compelling?
3.  What are some of the greatest challenges facing the Muslim faith today?
4.  Do you think it is important for Westerners to understand Islam?
5.  What are the principles of Islam that you like the most? The least? Why?
6.  What aspects of your culture or religion are misunderstood? What can be done to change that?

7. Do you believe that Judaism, Christianity, and Islam convey the same underlying messages?

8. Do you think that mutual tolerance between the Judeo-Christian West and the Muslim world is achievable?

9. What can Muslims do to improve their image?

# Chronology of Events

As mentioned in the prologue, this book is not a detailed account of historical facts and dates. However, the following chronology serves as a broad outline of the major events that have impacted the Muslim world over the centuries. As not all of these events are discussed in the text, the chronology is placed at the end of the book.

### THE LIFE OF THE PROPHET MUHAMMAD: c. 570–632

- c. 570: Birth of Muhammad in Mecca. His full name was Muhammad ibn Abdullah ibn abdel-Muttalib ibn Hashim. His mother, Amina, died when he was six, while his father died months before he was born. No one really knows when the Prophet was actually born, but 570 is the most commonly used date by Muslim scholars. He had no brothers or sisters.

- 610: First verses of the Quran revealed in a small cave near Mecca.
- 612: Officially starts preaching the message of Islam.
- 621: Experiences his transcendental voyage where he's placed in the presence of God (*al-Israa wal-Miaraaj*).
- 622: Migration to Medina (the hijra).
- 624: Changes the direction of Muslims' prayer (the qibla) from Jerusalem to Mecca. Muslims inflict a major defeat on the Quraysh of Mecca at the Battle of Badr.
- 625: Muslims suffer a severe defeat at the hands of the Meccans at the Battle of Uhud.
- 627: Battle of the Trench.
- 628: Muhammad's extraordinary peace initiative results in the Treaty of Hudaybiyya between Mecca and Medina.
- 630: Victory over the Quraysh and the Muslim occupation of Mecca.
- 631: Delivers his Farewell Sermon on Mount Arafat.
- 632: Dies in Medina on Monday, June 6 in the presence of his closest wife, Aisha, at the approximate age of sixty-two. The cause of death is unknown, although it has been documented that he experienced severe headaches for many months before passing on.

## THE RASHIDUN CALIPHS: 632–661

- 632–634: Abou Bakr al-Sudeeq—the beginning of the Islamic Caliphate.
- 634–644: Omar ibn al-Khattab.
- 644–656: Othman ibn Affan.
- 656–661: Ali ibn abi Talib.

## THE UMAYYAD CALIPHATE IN DAMASCUS: 661–750

- 661–680: Muawiya I moves his capital from Medina to Damascus. Hassan and Hussain ibn Ali, the grandsons of the Prophet, are brutally murdered by the Shia in what is present-day Iraq.
- 691: The Dome of the Rock and al-Aqsa Mosque are built in Jerusalem. After the Masjid al-Haram in Mecca and the Mosque of the Prophet in Medina, al-Aqsa is the third holiest site in Islam.
- 711: Conquest of Spain.
- 717–718: Attempt to conquer Constantinople.
- 732: Battle of Tours.
- 750: Umayyads are overthrown by the Abbasids, and move to Spain to establish the Cordoba Caliphate.

## THE ABBASID CALIPHATE IN BAGHDAD: 750–1258

- 750: Abou el-Abas takes power.
- 750–850: The four Sunni schools of Islamic law are established: Hanafi, Shafii, Malaki, and Hanbali.
- 751: The Arab-Muslims learn papermaking from the Chinese.
- 765: The Palace of Wisdom is built in Baghdad.
- 840–1200: The Golden Age of Islam.
- 875: Sharia law is formalized by Muslim scholars.
- 969: Al-Azhar University is founded in Cairo.
- 1055–1250: Expansion of Islam under the Seljuk-Turks.
- 1095: Pope Urban preaches the First Crusade.
- 1099: The Crusaders conquer Jerusalem.

♦ 1187: Saladin defeats the Crusaders at the Battle of Hattin and restores Jerusalem to Islam.

♦ 1258: The Mongols sack Baghdad. With the fall of the Abbasids, the Islamic Caliphate comes to an end.

### THE CORDOBA CALIPHATE IN SPAIN: 756–1031

### THE FATIMID CALIPHATE IN CAIRO: 910–1171

### TAMERLANE (TIMUR-I LANG) ESTABLISHES HIS EMPIRE IN PERSIA, IRAQ, AND SYRIA: 1379–1401

### THE AFSHARID AND SAFAVID DYNASTIES IN PERSIA: 1501–1796

### THE MUGHAL EMPIRE IN INDIA: 1526–1707

### THE OTTOMAN EMPIRE: 1299–1924

♦ 1299–1326: Othman I.

♦ 1453: Constantinople is conquered.

♦ 1520–1566: Suleiman II the Magnificent.

♦ 1683: The Ottomans fail in their second siege of Vienna.

♦ 1798–1962: French colonization of the Middle East (intermittent).

♦ 1803–1813: The extremist Wahhabis occupy the Arabian Hijaz (in present-day Saudi Arabia), taking it from Ottoman control.

♦ 1854–1856: The Crimean War, which arises from European rivalry over the protection of Christian minorities in the Ottoman Empire.

- 1882–1952: British colonization of the Middle East.
- 1897: The first Zionist conference is held in Basel. Its ultimate goal is to create a Jewish state in the Ottoman province of Palestine.
- 1914: The Ottoman Empire enters World War I.
- 1917: The Balfour Declaration formally gives British support to the creation of a Jewish homeland in Palestine.
- 1918: World War I ends.
- 1924: The Ottoman Empire comes to an end.

### POST-OTTOMAN EMPIRE

- 1928: Turkey is declared a secular state by Mustafa Kemal Ataturk. Hassan el-Banna establishes the Muslim Brotherhood in Egypt.
- 1932: Kingdom of Saudi Arabia established.
- 1935: Iran becomes the official name of Persia.
- 1936: Increased Jewish immigration provokes widespread Arab-Jewish fighting in Palestine.
- 1939: World War II starts.
- 1940s: The Muslim Brotherhood becomes the most powerful political force in Egypt.
- 1943: Beginning of Zionist campaigns in Palestine.
- 1945: World War II ends.
- 1948: Creation of the State of Israel. Arab armies suffer defeat in war with Israel.
- 1967: Six-Day War between Israel and its neighbors.
- 1972: Palestinian terrorists' killing of eleven Israeli athletes during the 1972 Summer Olympics in Munich.

- 1973: Arab oil embargo and the Yom Kippur War between Egypt/Syria and Israel.
- 1975: Islamic finance launched in Dubai.
- 1978: Egypt and Israel sign the Camp David Peace Accords.
- 1978–1979: The Iranian Revolution. Ayatollah Khomeini becomes the supreme leader of the Islamic Republic of Iran.
- 1979–1981: American hostages are held prisoner in the US embassy in Tehran. Soviet army invades Afghanistan.
- 1980: Beginning of the Iran-Iraq War.
- 1981: President Anwar Sadat of Egypt is assassinated by Muslim extremists.
- 1982–1985: Israel invades Lebanon.
- 1983: US and French military barracks bombed in Beirut.
- 1988: Osama bin Laden establishes al-Qaeda in Afghanistan.
- 1989: Before he dies, Ayatollah Khomeini issues a bizarre fatwa against the British author Salman Rushdie for his allegedly blasphemous portrayal of the Prophet Muhammad in his novel *The Satanic Verses*. The fatwa is unanimously condemned by Muslim countries as being un-Islamic. Iran-Iraq War comes to an end. Last Soviet soldiers leave Afghanistan.
- 1990: Military annexation of Kuwait by Iraq (under Saddam Hussein) is reversed in 1991 by a coalition of US-led forces.
- 1992–1994: Serbian and Croatian Christian nationalists systematically kill and force the Muslim inhabitants of Srebrenica in Bosnia to leave their homes.

- 1994: The Taliban extremists come to power in Afghanistan.
- 2001: Al-Qaeda's 9/11 attacks on the World Trade Center and Pentagon. In retaliation, the US initiates a military campaign against al-Qaeda and the Taliban in Afghanistan.
- 2003: US-led invasion of Iraq.
- 2004: Madrid train bombings by al-Qaeda in retaliation against the US invasion of Iraq.
- 2005: Terrorist bombings in London, motivated by Britain's involvement in the Iraq War.
- 2006: Saddam Hussein executed.
- 2007–2009: Credit crisis causes worst global recession since the 1930s, significantly impacting the economy of Dubai in the UAE.
- 2009: Israel launches major attack on Hamas militants in Gaza. President Barack Obama addresses the Muslim world from Cairo University.
- 2009: King Abdullah of Saudi Arabia removes conservative religious figures from his government. Norah al-Faiz is named deputy minister of education, becoming the first woman ever appointed to a government position in Saudi Arabia. Switzerland bans the construction of minarets after a referendum.
- 2010: World's tallest building, Burj Khalifa, opens in Dubai. French parliament passes law banning burqas. Controversy over whether an Islamic center should be built near the lower Manhattan site of the 9/11 attacks. The last US combat brigade withdraws from Iraq.

♦ 2011: Because of deep frustrations with high unemployment, inflation, and rampant corruption, weeks of protests in the streets of Tunisia escalated to the point where President Zine el-Abidine Ben Ali—who ruled the country for twenty-three years—had to flee the country. Inspired by the revolt in Tunisia, Egyptians held unprecedented demonstrations that led to the fall of the thirty-year regime of President Hosni Mubarak. In addition, as a result of the Libyan civil war, the dictatorial regime of Muammar Gaddafi, which lasted for forty-two years, ends. The "Arab Spring" revolutions in Tunisia, Egypt, and Libya trigger widespread political uncertainty in North Africa and the Middle East, especially in Syria and Yemen. Osama bin Laden is killed by US Navy Seals in Pakistan.

# Notes

Quotations from the Quran are from T. Cleary, *The Quran: A New Translation* (Burr Ridge, IL: Starlatch Press, 2004).

### PROLOGUE

1. The controversial documentary film, the name of which I won't mention, was produced in the US in 2006. The documentary claims that Islam is a violent religion that's bent on world domination. Critics of the film describe it as inaccurate, simplistic, biased, and propagandist against Islam.

### MYTH ONE: ISLAM CAME TO ERASE OTHER RELIGIONS

1. Quran: 87:14–19.
2. Ibid., 2:62.
3. The Pew Forum on Religion & Public Life, *Mapping the Global Muslim Population: A Report on the Size and Distribution of the*

*World's Muslim Population,* Washington, DC: Pew Research Center, (2009), 1

4. Quran: 3:52. The paramount notion of submitting to God in Islam is also conveyed in 3:19 of the Quran, which says: *"The religion before God is submission to His will."*

5. Ibid., 5:48.

6. Ibid., 51:56.

7. Based on a study conducted in 2002 by the Human Population Laboratories of the Public Health Institute and the California Department of Health Services, in conjunction with the University of California–Berkeley. The study was published in the April 4, 2002 edition of the *International Journal of Psychiatry in Medicine.*

8. M. Mokhtar and F. Ibrahim, the University of Malaya's Biomedical Engineering Department, Kuala Lumpur, Malaysia. *Assessment of Salat Taraweeh and Fasting Effect on Body Composition* (2008), http://www.springerlink.com/content/v8g470884165569j. html, (accessed November 14, 2009).

9. Quran: 109:6.

10. The SWOT Analysis technique is credited to Albert Humphrey, who led a research project at Stanford University in the 1970s using data from Fortune 500 companies.

11. M. Hart, *The 100: A Ranking of the Most Influential Persons in History* (New York: Citadel Press, 1998), 3–10.

12. Quran: 2:256.

13. Ibid., 5:48.

14. Ibid., 21:107.

15. Ibid., 5:19.

16. Ibid., 88:21.

17. Ibid., 7:158.

18. The Pew Forum.

19. Quran: 50:16.

## MYTH TWO: THE QURAN IS NOT A MIRACLE

1. Quran: 96:1–5.
2. All the quotes in this paragraph are from the hadith reported by al-Bukhari, vol. 1, book 1, no. 3 in the Arabic edition.
3. Ibid., no. 2 in the Arabic edition.
4. Quran: 15:9.
5. Ibid., 2:106.
6. Ibid., 16:101–102.
7. Some controversial sources claim that the total number of abrogated verses in the Quran is 246. For argument's sake, even if that's the total, the abrogated verses would comprise only 3.9 percent of all the verses in the Quran.
8. Quran: 17:86.
9. 9. A. Guillaume, *Life of Muhammad: A Translation of Ibn Ishaq's Sirat Rasul Allah* (Oxford: Oxford University Press, 1955), 165. For an in-depth discussion of the so-called satanic verses, also see K. Armstrong, *Muhammad: A Biography of the Prophet* (San Francisco: HarperCollins Publishers, 1993), 108–133.
10. Quran: 53:19–20.
11. K. Armstrong, *Islam: A Short History* (New York: The Modern Library, 2002), 5.
12. Quran: 24:35.
13. Ibid., 81:1–19.

Other capturing verses (Ibid., 21:30–35) include:

> *Don't the skeptics see*
> *that the skies and the earth used to be*
> *one solid mass,*
> *then We split them,*
> *and made all living things from water?*
> *Now won't they believe?*
> *And We put mountains on the earth*
> *lest it quake with them*
> *and We made passes through the mountains for roads*
> *that they may find their way.*

*And We made the sky a protected roof;*
*yet they still turn away from Our signs.*
*God is the one who created*
*the night and the day,*
*and the sun and the moon,*
*each floating in an orbit.*
*And we never granted immortality*
*to any human before you.*
*Every living being tastes death:*
*We first try you with ill and good as a test;*
*and then you shall be returned to Us.*

14. Ibid., 23:12–14.
15. Hadith reported by al-Bukhari, vol. 8, book 77, no. 59 in the Arabic edition.
16. In verse 79:30, the Quran mentions that the earth is slightly oval-shaped. The Arabic word *dahhaha* that's used in the verse means "oval-shaped." Dahhaha is derived from the word *duhiya* which specifically refers to the egg of an ostrich, which is oval and geospherical in shape, looking similar to a pumpkin. The earth isn't quite spherical, due to what's known as "rotational flattening," so it's shaped more like a pumpkin. The circumference of the earth at the equator is 24,902 miles; at the poles it's a bit shorter with 24,860 miles, so it's slightly wider than it's tall, giving it a slight bulge at the equator. It was Isaac Newton who first noted that the earth is not spherical, but slightly oval in shape. Moreover, the Quran says in verse 6:125

*"...Whomever God wishes to guide,*
*God opens his chest to surrender [Islam];*
*and whomever God wishes to delude,*
*God makes his chest narrow, contracted,*
*as if he were climbing up to the sky."*

It is a known scientific fact that as elevation rises to more than 12,000 feet, atmospheric pressure goes down as the atmosphere becomes thinner. Therefore, the amount of oxygen entering the bloodstream declines. As the air sacs in the lungs grow narrow and contract, we feel as if we cannot breathe. This scientific fact, which was unknown to Muhammad in the seventh century, appears to be explained in the verse above.

For additional scientific facts that are mentioned in the Quran, also see I. Ibrahim's *A Brief Illustrated Guide to Understanding Islam* (Houston: Darussalam, 2002), 5–31, as well as C. Taslaman's *The Quran: Unchallengeable Miracle* (Eden, SD: Nettleberry, 2006), 27–414.

17. Quran: 83:9 and 20.
18. A. Noufal, *Al-eagaaz al-adadee lill-Quran al-kareem* (or *The Numerical Miracles of the Quran*) (Cairo: Dar Akhbar al-Yom, 1975), 54–61.
19. Please refer to appendix A for the ninety-nine names of God that are mentioned in the Quran.
20. Quran: 89:27–30.
21. There are some thirty English translations of the Quran. I believe the most accurate translation is by T. Cleary, *The Quran: A New Translation* (Burr Ridge, IL: Starlatch Press, 2004), which, as mentioned at the beginning of the end notes, has been used to complete this book.

In terms of the interpretation of Quranic verses and the chronology of their revelation, the most widely used is A. Ali's classic *The Quran: Translation* (New York: Tahrike Tarsile Quran, 2000). A. Ali's translation was originally published in Lahore, Pakistan, in 1938.

For a complete list of the translated names of the 114 chapters of the Quran, please refer to appendix B.

22. Quran: 2:23 and 3:7.
23. Ibid., 41:53.

## MYTH THREE: THE PROPHET MUHAMMAD BASKED IN SENSUAL DELIGHT

1. M. Abou Daoud, *The Identity of the Prophet Muhammad ibn Abdullah* (Damascus: Most Rare Group, 2007), 8–26.
2. Hadith reported by al-Bukhari, vol. 5, book 58, no. 23 in the Arabic edition.
3. R. Haylamaz, "At what age did Aisha marry the Prophet?" *The Fountain* 69: 40–45.
4. Ibid.
5. Ibid.
6. Hadith reported by al-Bukhari, vol. 7, book 62, no. 64 in the Arabic edition, as follows:

"Narrated Aisha: 'The Prophet engaged me when I was a girl of six years. We went to Medina and stayed at the house of family friends. Then I got ill and my hair fell down. Later on my hair grew again and my mother came to me while I was playing on a swing with some of my girlfriends. She called me, and I went to her not knowing what she wanted to do to me. She caught me by the hand and made me stand at the door of the house. I was breathless then, and when my breathing became all right, she took some water and rubbed my face and head with it. Then she took me into the house. There in the house, I saw some women who said, "Best wishes, God's blessings, and good luck." Then she entrusted me to them and they prepared me for the betrothal. Unexpectedly, God's Apostle came to me in the forenoon and my mother handed me over to him, and at that time I was a girl of nine years of age.'"

According to the *Encyclopedia of Islam*, Boston: Brill, 2002, the earliest standard classical reference on the science of hadith was Abou Muhammad al-Ramahurmuzi's *Al-muhaddith al-faasil bayn al-rawi wa al-waee* (or *The Hadith Scholar That Differentiates Between the Narrator and the Aware*) written before he died in 971, while other significant work was Al-Hakim al-Naysaburi's *Maarifat ulum al-hadith* (or *Discovering the Science of Hadith*) and Ibn al-Salah's *Ulum al-hadith* (or *The Science of Hadith*), written between the years 1025 and 1240, respectively.

Although a *sahih* saying is in essence an obligatory one which must be acted upon according to the consensus of Islamic scholarship, Muslims are still allowed to analyze, debate, and (if possible) update the interpretation of a narration by the Prophet based on additional reliable sources of information attained after the death of the likes of al-Bukhari. This is known as tajdid or ijtihad (mentioned in chapter 9).

In reference to the specific hadith recorded by al-Bukhari in relation to Aisha's age at marriage, it is, however, now known (and based on recent research conducted by the contemporary Sheikh Khaled el-Gendy of Egypt) that one of the five sources in the chain of narrators was an old man of good reputation but with poor memory. According to al-Bukhari, there were five individuals in the chain of transmission for this specific hadith: Fazwa ibn abi al-Maghraa, Ali ibn Mashhar, Hisham, Abiya, and, lastly, Aisha. The research by Sheikh el-Gendy has brought to light that Hisham was an old man of around eighty who had a poor memory (probably Alzheimer's), and thus was not sure about the actual age of Aisha when she married the Prophet. Moreover, this narration, albeit categorized as sahih, lacks some coherence with additional and reliable information attained *after* the death of al-Bukhari.

In sum, al-Bukhari did his job correctly by accurately relaying what the narrators actually said, but in this specific case the content of what one individual in the chain of narrators conveyed appears to be slightly off-target.

7. Hadith reported by al-Bukhari, vol. 4, book 52, no. 12 in the Arabic edition.
8. Ibn Hisham, *Al-Sira al-Nabawiya* (or *The Biography of the Prophet*), vol. 1, 293–294 in the Arabic edition.
9. Ibid., 265–266.
10. G. Geyer, *When Cats Reigned Like Kings: On the Trail of the Sacred Cats* (Kansas City, MO: Andrews McMeel Publishing, 2004), 4.
11. Hadith reported by Ahmad, no. 12,117 in the Arabic edition.
12. Hadith narrated by Malik ibn Anas, vol. 49, no. 1.1 in the Arabic edition.

| | Summary Of Arabic Terms Related To The Hadith Of The Prophet | |
|---|---|---|
| **Arabic Term** | **Definition** | **Explanation/Comments** |
| *Hadith* | Oral anecdotes recalling the words and deeds of the Prophet Muhammad. | Single for *ahadith*. To simplify, I've used the word "hadith" throughout the book for both the singular and plural tense. |
| *Fiqh* | Islamic jurisprudence. | Pertains directly to Islamic law, or sharia. |
| *Sahih* | Correct, true, sound, or authentic. | To be accepted as sound and authentic, a hadith must meet specific technical requirements. The sahih sayings of the Prophet are those generally used as the sources of Islamic jurisprudence (fiqh), and are proof in cases involving Islamic law. When a hadith meets all the technical requirements for a sahih saying, it is expected to be accepted by all Muslims. If a hadith is believed to include one or more persons who had a weak memory (but were of good character and intentions), then it's called a *hassan* hadith. In other words, it's in a category that's below that of a sahih (authentic) saying. |
| *Daeef* | Weak and unsubstantiated. | It is unjustified to use a weak saying when a sahih one exists to present the actions and teachings of the Prophet. There are several reasons why a hadith is considered daeef, as mentioned below. |
| *Isnad* | Support and reliability for a chain of oral transmission. | To be a hadith sahih, the narration must first have an impeccable chain of transmission (isnad) in which there is no "missing link." Each link of the chain must have been connected by a narrator who actually heard the narration from the prior link in the chain, and so forth; while the chain of narrators must have been an unbroken chain. If one of the narrators who transmitted a hadith is missing, then it's called a *mursal* hadith, and is, therefore, considered to be daeef (weak). |

| *Aadel* | Just and honest person. | The second technical requirement for a hadith sahih. Each individual narrator must be a just (aadel) Muslim of good reputation. |
| *Matn* | Strength and consistency of the text and underlying meaning. | The third technical requirement for a hadith sahih. The underlying meaning of the text (matn) of the narration itself must be in accordance with Islamic teachings and in concert with the fundamental logic of Muhammad's known approaches to morality and ethics. In other words, the hadith must also pass a litmus test of basic common sense (i.e., Is it rational? Does all the information add up? Is the narration coherent with other reliable sources? Does the linguistic style coincide with the way the Prophet was known to have spoken?) |

13. M. Ames and D. Houston, "Legal, social, and biological definitions of pedophilia," *Archives of Sexual Behavior* 19: 553–563.

14. R. Wells, *Revolutions in Americans' Lives: A Demographic Perspective on the History of Americans, Their Families, and Their Society* (Westport, CT: Greenwood Publishing Group, 1982), 42.

15. The most trustworthy source for the reconstruction of the life of the historical Muhammad is the Quran. Next in importance are the traditional Muslim biographies of Muhammad and quotes attributed to him (i.e., Al-Sira al-Nabawiya and the hadith literature), which provide further details on Muhammad's approximately sixty-two-year life. The earliest surviving written biography is Ibn Ishaq's *Sirat Rasul Allah* (or *The Life of God's Messenger)* written some 130 years after the death of the Prophet. Although the original work is lost, portions of it survive in the subsequent work of Ibn Hisham (d. 833). Another early source is the history of Muhammad's campaigns by al-Waqidi (d. 822).

Other excellent sources include K. Armstrong, *Muhammad: A Biography of the Prophet* (New York: HarperCollins Publishers, 1993); M. Lings, *Muhammad: His Life Based on the Earliest Sources* (Rochester, VT: Inner Traditions, 2006); and T. Ramadan, *The Messenger: The Meanings of the Life of Muhammad* (London: Penguin Books, 2007).

## MYTH FOUR: WOMEN HAVE NO RIGHTS IN ISLAM

1. M. Zakzouk, *Islamic Facts: Refuting the Allegations Against Islam* (Cairo: Ministry of Religious Endowments for Preaching, 2002), 63–82.

2. Quran: 33:53.

3. Ibid., 24:31.

4. Ibid., 33:59.

5. Ibid., 33:33.

6. M. Gohari, *The Taliban: Ascent to Power* (Oxford: Oxford University Press, 2000), 108–110.

7. Zakzouk, *Islamic Facts*, 78.
8. Quran: 4:3.
9. Ibid., 4:129.
10. Ibid., 4:3.
11. Ibid., 4:11.

All the mandatory rules of inheritance in Islam are laid down in precise terms in verses 11–13 of chapter 4 ("Women") of the Quran, as well as in verses 225–242 of chapter 2 ("The Cow").

Also see *Ahkam al-tarika wal mawareth* (or *Islamic Laws of Legacies and Inheritance*) by the Egyptian Sheikh Muhammad Abou Zahra (Cairo, Al-Azhar University, 1964).

12. E. Hecker, *A Short History of Women's Rights* (Westport, CT: Greenwood Press, 1914), 125.
13. *The Status of Children and Women Report* by the Arab League and the UN Children's Fund, UNICEF, 2005.
14. Hadith reported by Ibn Majah, no. 2,771 in the Arabic edition.

## MYTH FIVE: ISLAM WAS SPREAD WITH THE SWORD

1. K. Armstrong, *Islam: A Short History* (New York: The Modern Library, 2002), 27.
2. Quran: 109:6.
3. J. Esposito, *Islam: The Straight Path* (New York: Oxford University Press, 1998), 34.
4. United Nations Sub-Commission on the Prevention of Discrimination and Protection of Minorities, 1985.
5. J. McCarthy, *The Armenians in the Late Ottoman Period* (Ankara: The Turkish Historical Society for the Council of Culture, Arts, and Publications, 2001), 65–86.

6. Most names and dates in this section are from M. Morgan, *Lost History: The Enduring Legacy of Muslim Scientists, Thinkers, and Artists* (Washington, DC: National Geographic, 2008).

7. A. de Libera, *Averroès et l'averroïsme* (Paris: PUF, 1991), 121.

8. C. Haviland, "The roar of Rumi—800 years on," BBC News, September 30, 2007.

9. C. Barks, *The Essential Rumi* (New York: HarperCollins Publishers, 1995), 32.

10. Armstrong, *Islam*, 32.

11. D. O'Leary, *Islam at the Crossroads: A Brief Survey of the Present Position and Problems of the World of Islam* (New York: E. P. Dutton, 1923), 8.

12. Mark Glenn is writer/commentator and a frequent contributor to *The March Media Resources*, as well as other online media.

13. M. Zakzouk, *Islamic Facts: Refuting the Allegations Against Islam* (Cairo: Ministry of Religious Endowments for Preaching, 2002), 32.

## MYTH SIX: ISLAM IS AN INHERENTLY HOSTILE AND INTOLERANT FAITH

1. Quran: 10:25 and 5:2.

2. Ibid., 5:32.

Another relevant verse in this chapter, which was revealed when the Prophet was migrating to Medina in 622, is: *"And fight back for the sake of God those who fight you; but do not be brutal or commit aggression, for God does not love brutal aggressors."* Quran: 2:190.

3. Ibid., 2:256.

4. Ibid., 9:1–6.

5. M. al-Tamimi, *Provisions of the Hereafter* (Translated and abridged from Ibn al-Qayyem al-Jawziyya's *Zaad el-meaad fi khayr hadye al-ebaad*) (Birmingham, England: Darussalam, 2003), 323–356.

6. Ibid.
7. Ibrahim, "America and the Muslim world must change their love-hate relationship," in Nimer, *Islamophobia and Anti-Americanism: Causes and Remedies* (Beltsville, MD: Amana Publications, 2007), 38.

In 1997, the Runnymede Trust, a British think tank, coined the term "Islamophobia" to capture the growing animosity toward Muslims in the West.

8. M. Zakzouk, *Islamic Facts: Refuting the Allegations Against Islam* (Cairo: Ministry of Religious Endowments for Preaching, 2002), 39.
9. Quran: 22:39.
10. Ibid., 2:194.
11. Ibid., 8:61.
12. Ibid., 60:8.
13. Hadith reported by al-Bukhari, vol. 8, book 73, no. 73 in the Arabic edition.
14. Ibid.
15. Quran: 4:29–30.
16. M. Sutton, "Appendix: Statistical Summary," in *Bear in Mind These Dead: An Index of Deaths from the Conflict in Ireland 1969–1993* (Belfast: Beyond the Pale Publications, 1994).
17. R. Moore, *A Sympathetic History of Jonestown* (Lewiston, NY: The Edwin Mellen Press, 1985), xvi.
18. K. Newport, *The Branch Davidians of Waco: The History and Beliefs of an Apocalyptic Sect* (New York: Oxford University Press, 2006), 1.
19. Ron Suskind, "Faith, Certainty and the Presidency of George W. Bush," *The New York Times Magazine* (New York), October 17, 2004.
20. Based on data compiled between March 2003 and April 2010 by the Iraq Body Count project (IBC). The data was attained from the IBC's web site http://www.iraqbodycount.org/database/ (accessed May 25, 2010).

21. Paul Harris, "Bush Says God Chose Him to Lead His Nation," *The Observer* (London), November 2, 2003.

22. Ibid.

23. M. Bohn, *The Achille Lauro Hijacking: Lessons in the Politics and Prejudice of Terrorism* (Dulles, VA: Brassey's, 2004), 67, 176–177.

24. Avi Issacharoff, "Settlers Remember Gunman Goldstein; Hebron Riots Continue," *Haaretz* (Tel Aviv), February 28, 2010.

25. Yaakov Lappin, "IDF Releases Cast Lead Casualty," *The Jerusalem Post*, March 26, 2009. ("IDF" refers to the Israeli Defense Forces).

26. Maqbool, "Scale of Gaza destruction emerges," BBC News, January 19, 2009.

27. Amos Harel, "IDF Rabbinate Publication During Gaza War: We Will Show No Mercy On The Cruel," *Haaretz* (Tel Aviv), January 26, 2009.

28. J. Ching, *Genocide and the Bosnian War* (New York: The Rosen Publishing Group, 2009), 6. (The estimated number of Muslims killed during the Bosnian Genocide varies by source).

29. J. Renard, *101 Questions and Answers on Islam* (New York: Gramercy Books, 1998), 140.

30. Ibid.

31. Quran: 49:13.

## MYTH SEVEN: JUDAISM IS THE ENEMY OF ISLAM

1. Quran 5:44 and 46.

2. S. Mubarakpuri, *al-Raheeq al-Makhtoom* (or *The Sealed Nectar*) (Medina: Dar al-Salaam Publications: 2002), 147–150.

3. Quran: 29:46.

4. Hadith reported by al-Bukhari, vol. 2, book 23, no. 399 in the Arabic edition.

5. P. Holt, A. Lambton, and B. Lewis, *Cambridge History of Islam: The Indian Sub-Continent, Southeast Asia, Africa, and the Muslim West* (Cambridge: Cambridge University Press, 1977), 47–48.

6. M. Lings, *Muhammad: His Life Based on the Earliest Sources* (Rochester, VT: Inner Traditions, 2006), 215.

7. C. Glassé, *The New Encyclopedia of Islam: Revised Edition of the Concise Encyclopedia of Islam* (Lanham, MD: Rowman & Littlefield Publishers, 2008), 92.

8. M. Rodinson, *Muhammad: Prophet of Islam* (London: Tauris Parke, 2002), 209.

9. M. Watt, *Muhammad at Medina* (Oxford: Oxford University Press, 1956), 36.

The main source of the Battle of the Trench, or the Confederates, is the thirty-third chapter of the Quran (called al-Ahzab). Although the Quran doesn't speak directly about the events, it reveals the psychological and social situation of the people of Medina, coupled with the different feelings among them toward the battle.

10. F. Peters, *Muhammad and the Origins of Islam* (Albany, NY: State University of New York Press, 1994), 224.

11. S. Maududi, *The Meaning of the Quran*, trans. A. Kamal (Lahore: Islamic Publications, 1999), 64.

12. Lings, *Muhammad*, 221–223.

13. D. Peterson, *Muhammad: Prophet of God* (Grand Rapids, MI: Wm. B. Eerdmans Publishing, 2007), 123.

14. Lings, *Muhammad*, 224–226.

15. Ibn Hisham, *Al-Sira al-Nabawiya*, vol. 4. 188 in the Arabic edition.

16. Lings, *Muhammad*, 221–223.

17. Ibid., 227.

18. T. Ramadan, *The Messenger: The Meanings of the Life of Muhammad* (New York: Penguin Books, 2007), 145.

19. Ibid.

20. Ibid.

21. Ibid., 146.

22. Ibid.

23. Ibid.

24. Ibid.

25. Ibid.

26. Ibid.
27. K. Armstrong, *Islam: A Short History* (New York: The Modern Library, 2002).
28. Ibid.
29. Ibid.
30. Such groups include: True Torah Jews Against Zionism, Jews Not Zionists, and Neturei Karta.
31. A. Bostom, *The Legacy of Islamic Anti-Semitism: From Sacred Texts to Solemn History* (Amherst, NY: Prometheus Books, 2008), 31.
32. Ibid.
33. Ibid.
34. Armstrong, *Islam*, 21.
35. Ibid., 22.
36. Quran: 19:51–52.

## MYTH EIGHT: CHRISTIANITY IS THE ENEMY OF ISLAM

1. Quran: 3:48–49. The English translations of relevant portions of chapter 3 ("The Family of Amran") and chapter 19 ("Mary") of the Quran are provided in appendix C.
2. R. Du Pasquier, *Unveiling Islam*, trans. T. Winter (Cambridge, England: The Islamic Texts Society, 1992), 5.
3. J. Riley-Smith, *The Oxford History of the Crusades* (New York: Oxford University Press, 1999), 1–14.
4. B. Robinson, "About the Crusades and Their Legacy of Hatred," Ontario Consultants on Religious Tolerance, http://www.religioustolerance.org/chr_cru1.htm, (accessed February 9, 2010).
5. J. Riley-Smith, *The Atlas of the Crusades* (New York: Facts on File, 1990), 50–140.
6. Ibid.
7. Quran: 1:1–7.
8. T. Cleary, *The Quran: A New Translation* (Burr Ridge, IL: Starlatch Press, 2004).

In addition to Al-Fatiha, the fifty-first verse of the fifth chapter of the Quran (named "The Table") is also widely misinterpreted:

> *Believers, do not take*
> *the Jews and Christians for protecting allies (awliyaa);*
> *they are protecting allies of each other.*
> *And whoever chooses them is one of them.*
> *God does not guide people acting unjustly.*

It's beneficial to realize that there's no issue with Muslims having friendships and acquaintances with people of other faiths—as long as they don't violently oppose Muslims, don't wrongly influence them toward immoral behavior, and aren't unjust to others. This should set the general tone for how verse 5:51 is to be interpreted, as it has so often been misused to claim that Islam instructs its followers not to have any social relations with non-Muslims.

The verse above contains the word *awliyaa*, (which comes from the Arabic word *waali*). The mistranslation of awliyaa, without any further qualification or nuance, is what has caused the false allegations surrounding 5:51. Waali in the Arabic language has a wide set of meanings, none of which are used to mean "friend or acquaintance." In this verse, according to Sheikh Faraz Rabbani (a scholar and researcher of Islamic law), awliyaa means "protecting allies." It doesn't suggest "friend," where the impression that Muslims should be isolationists may be given. As such, Muslims can certainly forge friendships with non-Muslims who are positive toward them and supportive of their rights.

It's paramount to understand the context of the entire fifth chapter and the situations under which its fifty-first verse was revealed. Classical scholars of Quranic exegesis (*al-Tafseer* or *Asbaab al-nezool*) have indicated that 5:51 has several possible reasons for revelation.

In the last stages of the Prophet's life in Medina (627 to 632), the Muslims had emerged with their own unique social, economic, and political systems. At the same time, the polytheists of Mecca, as well as the Jews and Christians of Arabia, had established their own independent socioeconomic systems. Amid such an environment, the hypocrites among the Muslims maintained secret ties with specific groups of Jews and Christians, supporting them and seeking to broker deals that would harm the well-being of Muhammad's followers. It's in this context that the Quran revealed 5:51, specifically admonishing these hypocrites among the Muslims not to take the Jews and Christians (who wanted Islam's newly established systems to fail) as protecting allies. In addition, 5:51 uses the words "the Jews" and "the Christians," making it clear that it's only a *specific* group of Jews and Christians the Quran is actually referring to. In other words, the verse isn't a blanket prescription for *all* members of the two other divine faiths.

9. Quran: 3:3.
10. J. Renard, *101 Questions and Answers on Islam* (New York: Gramercy Books, 1998), 106.
11. Ibid.
12. Ibid., 107.
13. Ibid.
14. Ibid.
15. Muslim scholars tend to believe that the Injil (from the Greek *evangel* or "gospel") spoken of by the Quran is not the New Testament. Rather, it is the single gospel which, Islam teaches, was revealed to Jesus, and which he taught himself. Fragments of it survive in the four canonical Gospels and in some others, of which traces survive (i.e., the Gospel of the Nativity). Muslims, therefore, reject the Nicene Creed dogma of Christianity.

In addition to the Injil, the Jewish Torah (*al-Taurah* in Arabic) is frequently referred to in the Quran. Muslim tradition names the Torah as "The Law," or the Jewish scripture that was based on the original teachings of Moses. Al-Taurah is mentioned with great honor in the Quran as having been, in its purity, a true revelation from God (*Yahweh, El,* or *Elohim* in old Hebrew). Muslims believe that the Old Testament is not the original Torah, as it includes a mass of traditional writings that were added to the original Torah around 400 BC, after the return of the Jews from Babylonian captivity. In

Islam, the Old Testament is considered a Christian term applied to a body of old Jewish records.

The above text and interpretation is adapted from A. Ali's *The Quran: Translation* (New York: Tahrike Tarsile Quran, 2000), 282–287.

16. Quran: 112.
17. K. Armstrong, *A History of God: The 4,000-Year Quest of Judaism, Christianity and Islam* (New York: Ballantine, 1993), 60.
18. Quran: 5:116–117.
19. Ibid., 61:6.
20. J. Crossan, *Jesus: A Revolutionary Biography* (San Francisco: HarperCollins Publishers, 1989), 201.
21. "Arianism," *The Catholic Encyclopedia*, vol. 11, (New York: Robert Appleton Company, 1909), 5–9.
22. Armstrong, *A History*, 110–113.
23. Ibid. Translated from the Latin copy called the *Missale Romanum*. The Latin version was translated from the original Nicene Creed that was written in Greek, which was actually composed at the Council of Constantinople in 381.

   Also see M. Baigent's *The Jesus Papers: Exposing the Biggest Cover-Up in History* (San Francisco: HarperCollins Publishers, 2003).

24. *The Panarion of Epiphanius of Salamis*, trans. F. Williams (Leiden, the Netherlands: Brill, 1994), 319–585.
25. Quran: 4:157–158.
26. Renard, *101 Questions*, 108.
27. Ibid., 114.
28. Ibid., 115.

## MYTH NINE: ISLAM IS INCOMPATIBLE WITH WESTERN MODERNITY

1. Hadith reported by al-Tirmidhi, no. 74 in the Arabic edition.
2. Quran: 96:1 and 4–5.

3. *Arab Human Development Report* (AHDR) by the UN Development Program, 2002–2005.

4. Ibid.

5. Ibid., and the World Bank (2008 data).

6. Quran: 2:222.

7. Ibid., 2:219.

8. J. Renard, *101 Questions and Answers on Islam* (New York: Gramercy Books, 1998), 138.

9. M. El-Gamal, *Overview of Islamic Finance* (Cairo: Department of the Treasury's Office of International Affairs 2006), 1.

10. Renard, *101 Questions*, 137.

11. Ibid.

12. Ibid.

13. Ibid., 138.

14. Ibid.

15. Ibid.

16. Merrill Lynch, *Global Economics* (London: Merrill Lynch, 2008), 16.

17. The Central Bank of Egypt.

18. H. Kassim, *Legitimizing Modernity in Islam: Muslim Modus Vivendi and Western Modernity* (Lewiston, NY: The Edwin Mellen Press, 2005), 4.

19. For a complete list of member countries of the Organization of the Islamic Conference (OIC), see the web site: http://www. oic-oci.org/.

20. Quran: 5:38–39.

21. D. Wiechman, J. Kendall, and M. Azarian, "Islamic law: Myths and realities," http://muslim-canada.org/Islam_myths.htm, (accessed January 8, 2010). The article was originally published by the Office of International Criminal Justice of the University of Illinois–Chicago in September 2005.

22. Quran: 17:32.

23. Ibid., 24:2 and 4–5.

24. M. Zakzouk, *Islamic Facts: Refuting the Allegations Against Islam* (Cairo: Ministry of Religious Endowments for Preaching, 2002), 55–59.

25. Ibid.

26. Quran: 3:159.

27. Zakzouk, *Islamic Facts*, 55–59.

28. Ibid.

29. Ibid.

30. It is most encouraging to know that in March 2010, the influential Pakistani scholar Dr. Tahir ul-Qadri issued a 600-page fatwa against terrorism and suicide bombing. In his religious ruling, delivered in London, Dr. Qadri clearly indicated that Islam forbids the massacre of innocent citizens and suicide bombings. Such a stance is urgently needed from Muslim scholars around the world.

31. J. Esposito, *The Future of Islam* (New York: Oxford University Press, 2010), 198.

32. Quran: 13:11.

## EPILOGUE

1. Quran: 7:204–205.

2. Survey conducted in 2006 and 2007 by the National Center for Social Research, based in London, England.

3. Survey conducted in 2001 by the Barna Group, based in Ventura, California.

4. The Institute for Social Research at the University of Michigan-Ann Arbor periodically conducts the *World Values Survey*. Between 1995 and 1997, Diane Swanbrow and Richard Ingelhart of the University of Michigan authored the "Study of worldwide rates of religiosity and church attendance." The quote by Richard Ingelhart is derived from this study, available at http://www.religioustolerance.org/rel_ratefor.htm, (accessed October 27, 2009).

5. From an interview with Christiane Amanpour of CNN on November 10, 2009.

6. The nationwide survey conducted in 2008 of over four thousand adults found that 38 percent of those polled believed Islam was more likely than other faiths to encourage violence, down from the 45 percent who held this view two years earlier. The survey also found that 58 percent of Americans believe that Muslims face a lot of discrimination in the US.

7. Hadith reported by Ahmad, no. 19,774 in the Arabic edition.

# Glossary of Arabic Terms

**abaya:** A cloak or over-garment worn by some women in parts of the Islamic world. A long-sleeved, robe-like dress, it is the traditional form of Islamic attire for many countries of the Arabian Peninsula, such as Saudi Arabia and the United Arab Emirates. It has nothing to do with Islamic teachings.

**abi:** Means "father of" in an Arabic name. For example, the name Ali ibn abi Talib is directly translated as "Ali the son of the father of Talib." The word "ibn," which means "son" can also be written as "bin."

**al:** Means "the." It also can be written as "el."

**Allah:** God. Derived from the word *al-Ilah* which means "the one and only god." It is used by Arabic-speakers of all Abrahamic religions, including Jews and Christians, in reference to God. The term was also used by polytheist Meccans as a reference to a creator-god, possibly the supreme deity in pre-Islamic Arabia.

**Ashoura:** According to **Sunni** (s.v.) Muslim tradition, Muhammad fasted on this day. He asked Muslims to fast in honor of Moses, who fasted on that day (Passover) to express gratitude to God for liberating the Israelites from Egypt. Ashoura is also the tenth day of Muharram in the Islamic calendar. It is commemorated by **Shia** (s.v.) Muslims as a day of mourning for the martyrdom of Hussain ibn Ali, the grandson of the Prophet, at the Battle of Karbala (in present-day Iraq) on 10 Muharram in 680.

**awra:** Certain parts of the body, for both men and women, which are to be covered with clothing. Exposing the awra is unlawful in Islam and is regarded by some scholars as a sin. The exact definition of awra varies between the different schools of Islamic thought.

**al-Ahzab:** The Confederates, clans, coalition, or combined forces. The name of the thirty-third chapter in the Quran, which refers directly to the coalition of Meccan polytheists and three powerful Jewish tribes (Nadir, Qaynuqa, and Qurayza) that planned to eliminate Muhammad and his followers at the Battle of the Trench that took place near Medina in 627.

**al-Ameen:** The honest one. The name was given by Meccans to Muhammad before he became a prophet, because of his honesty in dealings as a merchant.

**al-Andalus:** Parts of the Iberian Peninsula (Andalusia) governed by Arab and North African Muslims (the Moors) between 711 and 1492.

**al-Ansar:** The victors. It refers to the inhabitants of Medina who welcomed and supported the Prophet when he arrived in Medina in 622.

**Al-Fatiha:** Name of the first chapter of the Quran. It means "The Opening."

**al-Fuqahaa:** Experts and scholars of **fiqh** (s.v.), or Islamic jurisprudence. A similar word is *ulamaa.*

**al-Jahiliyya:** Period of "dark ignorance" and intertribal conflict that plagued Arabia before the advent of Islam.

**al-Rawda al-Nabawiya:** Small area in the Mosque of the Prophet in Medina, located next to his house, pulpit, and tomb.

**al-Shahada:** The Muslim declaration of belief in the oneness of God and the acceptance of Muhammad as His prophet. The declaration reads, "La ilaha illa Allah, Muhammad Rasul Allah" ("There is no god but God, and Muhammad is the Messenger of God").

**al-shuaraa:** The poets. Muslims believe that the Quran was delivered during an era when poetry (*sheare*) was so highly regarded in order to prove to the inhabitants of Arabia that the Quran is a miracle, given the exquisite quality of its language.

**al-Taurah:** The Torah.

**Bani Israeel:** The Children of Israel, as mentioned in the Quran. A similar word is "Banu," as in Banu Nadir (the Jewish tribe of Medina). The Arabic term for Jews is *yahud,* the singular of which is *yahudi.*

**burqa:** A piece of clothing (typically black) that covers a woman from head to foot. There is an opening for the eyes, but the rest of the body (except the hands), is covered. The burqa is usually made of light fabric, and is essentially outerwear for some Muslim women in various regions. It is worn over their indoor clothes when women leave their homes. It's not worn indoors in the presence of immediate family members. The burqa originated in parts of present-day Afghanistan and Pakistan to protect young women from abusive men and the elements. It has nothing to do with Islamic teachings.

**caliph:** The successor to Muhammad and the temporal leader of the Muslim community.

**dhimmi:** Collectively *ahl al-dhimma,* or "the people of the dhimma," or "pact of protection." The word is derived from the Ottoman-Turkish and Urdu *zimmi,* or "one whose *zimma* (responsibility of protection) has been taken." A non-Muslim subject of a state governed in accordance with **sharia** (s.v.) law.

**dishdasha:** A white, ankle-length garment, usually with long sleeves and similar to a robe; also known as a *thawb.* It is worn by men in countries in the Arabian Peninsula. It's a type of attire that is cultural and has no connection to Islam.

**Eid al-Adha:** The "Festival of Sacrifice" or "Greater Eid." It is an important religious holiday celebrated by Muslims worldwide to commemorate the willingness of Abraham to sacrifice his son Ishmael as an act of obedience to God, which He rewarded by allowing him to sacrifice a ram instead.

**fard:** Obligatory teaching according to the **sharia** (s.v.), including the Five Pillars of Islam (accepting fully that God is the one and only God and that the Prophet Muhammad is one of His messengers, prayer, fasting, giving to the needy, and completing the pilgrimage to Mecca once in a lifetime). It is used interchangeably with the term **wajib** (s.v.).

**fatwa:** A religious opinion concerning **sharia** (s.v.) issued by an Islamic expert or scholar. In **Sunni** (s.v.) Islam, any fatwa is nonbinding, whereas in **Shia** (s.v.) Islam it could be considered by an individual as binding, depending on his or her relation to the scholar. The person who issues a fatwa is called a *mufti*. This is not necessarily a formal position, since most Muslims believe that anyone properly trained in Islamic law may give an opinion (fatwa) on its teachings. The term became notorious in the West after the Iranian Ayatollah Khomeini issued a strange fatwa against the British author Salman Rushdie for writing *The Satanic Verses*.

**fiqh:** An expansion of Islamic law based on the Quran and the **sunna** (s.v.) that complements **sharia** (s.v.) with evolving rulings and interpretations of Islamic jurists.

**gharaniq:** The name of a type of bird which is related to the so-called satanic verses in the Quran. The prevailing Muslim view of what is sometimes called the "gharaniq incident" by Muslim scholars is that it was a fabrication created by the unbelievers of Mecca in the early days of Islam.

**hadith:** Narrations originating from the words and deeds of the Prophet Muhammad. A hadith (single for *ahadith*) is regarded by traditional schools of jurisprudence as an important tool for understanding the Quran and the **sunna** (s.v.). Evaluated and gathered into large collections mostly during the reign of the caliph Omar ibn abdel-Aziz during the eighth century, these works are referred to in matters of Islamic law and history to this day. The most reliable source of hadith is al-Bukhari.

**hajj:** The pilgrimage to Mecca that each Muslim is required to complete once in a lifetime, but only if financially and physically able to do so.

**halal:** Lawful or legal; a term designating any object or action which is permissible to use or engage in according to Islamic law. The term is also used to designate food seen as permissible. It is the opposite of **haraam** (s.v.).

**Hanifs:** Pre-Islamic, non-Jewish, or non-Christian Arabian monotheists. They rejected *shirk* (polytheism) and retained some or all of the true tenets of the monotheist religion of Abraham (Ibrahim). The term is from the Arabic root *h-n-f* meaning "to decline," derived from the Syriac root of the same meaning.

**haraam:** Forbidden. In Islam it is used to refer to anything that is prohibited by the faith. Its antonym is **halal** (q.v.).

**hijab:** Commonly understood as a type of head covering (or veil) traditionally worn by Muslim women. Similar head coverings are wimples worn by Christian nuns and snoods often worn by married, Orthodox Jewish women. The word literally means "curtain" or "screen," based on the root meaning "to cover" or "to shelter." The correct word for a veil in the Quran is **khimar** (s.v.).

**hijra:** The emigration of the Prophet Muhammad and some seventy of his followers from Mecca to Medina in 622.

**hijri:** Islamic or hijri calendar. A lunar calendar based on twelve lunar months in a year of 354 or 355 days, used to date events in many Muslim countries (concurrently with the Gregorian calendar), and used by Muslims everywhere to determine the proper day on which to celebrate Islamic holy days and festivals. The first hijri year was the year during which the emigration of Muhammad from Mecca to Medina, known as the **hijra** (q.v.), took place.

**huffaz:** Prestigious title for those who have memorized the entire Quran.

**ihraam:** Sacred state which a Muslim must enter in order to perform the major pilgrimage or **hajj** (q.v.) or the minor pilgrimage (*umra*). A pilgrim must enter into this state before crossing the pilgrimage boundary near Mecca, known as the *miqaat*, by performing the cleansing rituals and wearing the prescribed attire.

**ijtihad:** Technical term of Islamic law that describes the process of making a legal decision by independent interpretation of the legal sources, the Quran, and the **sunna** (s.v.).

**ikrah:** Compulsion.

**imam:** An Islamic leadership position; often the leader of a mosque and the Muslim community. Similar to spiritual leaders, the imam is the one who leads the prayer during Islamic gatherings. Islam does not have a centralized religious authority (like a Pope), and teaches that God can be directly accessed by anyone without intermediation. **Shia** (s.v.) Muslims use the word *ayatollah* ("sign of God") as another word for imam.

**Injil:** The original teachings of Jesus. One of the five holy books that the Quran records as revealed by God, the others being the Scrolls of Abraham, the Zabur (of the Sabians), the Torah, and the Quran. Some Muslims believe that the New Testament was altered over time; others hold the view that the Injil is a lost book, different from the New Testament which was either written by the Christian apostles or people connected to them.

**iqraa:** Read (verb). It was the first word revealed by the Angel Gabriel to the Prophet in a small cave in Mount Nour near Mecca in 610. Some Muslim scholars interpret it as "recite."

**islah:** To repair; often translated as "to reform" or "reshape."

**jalabibihinna:** Outer garments of women. It is the feminine plural of the word *jilbab* which refers to any long and loose-fit coat or garment worn by some Muslim women. The modern jilbab covers the entire body, except for the hands, face, and head. The head and neck are then covered by a scarf, wrap, or veil (**khimar**, s.v.). It's mentioned in the Quran in 33:59.

**jeubihinna:** Feminine plural for the word *jeub* which means the chest, bosoms, or cleavage of a woman. It's mentioned in the Quran in 24:31.

**jihad:** A religious duty of Muslims and a noun meaning "to struggle" to improve oneself and/or society. Jihad appears frequently in the Quran and is interpreted by mainstream Muslims as "striving in the way to God." In its commonly misinterpreted context in the West, jihad means "holy war."

**jinn:** Demons, or genies. In Islam, the jinn are not fallen angels. They are believed to have been created from a "smokeless flame of fire" (Quran: 55:15). The first recorded jinn who was disobedient toward God is Iblis (Satan). Disbelieving and disobedient jinn are known as *shayateen*.

**jizya:** Per-capita tax that was levied on a section of an Islamic state's non-Muslim citizens (**dhimmis**, q.v.), who met certain criteria. The tax was levied on able-bodied adult males of military age and affording power, but with specific exemptions. Per-capita tax, which also was a sort of "fee" to protect non-Muslims from aggressors, was discarded at various points in history.

**juhd:** Effort or attempt to improve oneself and/or society. Directly related to **jihad** (q.v.).

**Kaaba:** Cube-shaped shrine in Mecca, Saudi Arabia, that's covered by a black silk and gold curtain known as the *kiswa*, which is replaced yearly and beautifully decorated with Quranic words. It is made of granite from the hills near Mecca, and stands upon a ten-inch marble base. The structure predates Islam, and according to Islamic tradition, the first shrine at the site was built by Abraham (although some Muslims believe that it was built by Adam). The structure has a vast mosque built around it, the Masjid al-Haram. All Muslims around the world face the Kaaba during prayers, no matter where they are. It is a symbol of the unity of the one and only God, and is the most sacred site in Islam. The Kaaba also has the Black Stone (*al-hajjar al-aswad*) placed into it. The Black Stone is an Arabian artifact which, according to Islamic tradition, dates back to the time of Adam and Eve, while some Western scientists believe that it's a tektite or a meteorite. It's placed in the eastern cornerstone of the Kaaba, and is approximately 42 inches tall and 18 inches wide.

**khimar:** Headscarf or wrap that can be used to cover the chest or cleavage of a woman. The Quran recommends that women draw their khimars (or more specifically *khumuri-hinna* in the plural feminine tense) to cover their chests for modesty. It is the technically correct word for a veil, which is more commonly known as **hijab** (q.v.). Sheikh Muhammad Metwally al-Sharaawy (d. 1998), the prolific Egyptian scholar of Quranic exegesis, explained that the khimar was initially short in length and only covered the head, but after the revelation of verse 24:31, Muslim women started to wear longer veils that were drawn further down to cover their chests.

**kitabun marqoum:** A numerically coded book. These words appear in the Quran (83:9 and 20). Some Muslims believe that they refer to the underlying mathematical balance of specific words that are revealed in the Quran.

**madrassa:** Any type of school, whether secular or religious.

**makruh:** A disliked or offensive act (literally, "hated"). Though it is not **haraam** (q.v.), and therefore not a sin, a person who abstains from this action is to be rewarded. Muslims are encouraged to avoid such actions when possible. This is one of the five degrees of approval (*ahkam*) in Islamic law.

**malayka:** Angels. The greatest angel in Islam is Jibreel (the Judeo-Christian Gabriel). Gabriel is the archangel who revealed the Quran to Muhammad—word by word, verse by verse. Gabriel is also known as the angel who communicates with all prophets. Mikaeel (Michael) is often depicted as the angel of mercy who is responsible for bringing rain and thunder to earth. He is also responsible for the rewards granted to good souls in this life. According to the hadith, Israfeel (Raphael) is responsible for signaling the coming of the day of judgment by "blowing a horn." The blowing of the horn is described in many places in the Quran. The Quran says that the first blow will destroy everything, while the second will bring all humans back to life again. Malak el-Mawt (Azrael) is responsible for parting the soul from the body. His name means the "angel of death" in Arabic. Other well-known angels in Islam include Maalik, the chief of the angels who governs hell; the Zabaniya, the nineteen angels who torment sinful souls in hell; the Dardaeel (the Journeyers), who travel the earth searching out assemblies where people remember God's name; and, lastly, Ridwan, the angel who oversees heaven (or *al-janna* in Arabic). In addition to the Five Pillars of Islam, Muslims are required to believe in all the angels, books, and prophets of God.

**mubah:** Denoting an action as being neither forbidden nor recommended and, therefore, religiously neutral. It is the most flexible category in Islamic law.

**mustahab:** Recommended, favored, or virtuous action.

**naskh:** Abrogation. It shares the same root as the words appearing in the phrase *al-nasikh wal mansukh* or "the abrogating and abrogated verses." In its Quranic application, naskh involves the replacement (*tabdil*) of an earlier verse (and thus its embodied ruling) with a chronologically successive and updated one.

**niqab:** Clothing which covers the entire body, worn by some Muslim women today. It is believed to have originally been part of women's dress among certain classes in the Byzantine Empire and/or pre-Islamic Persia, and adopted into Muslim culture during the Arab conquests of the Middle East. The niqab (or **burqa**, q.v.) is most common in the Arab countries of the Persian Gulf, such as Saudi Arabia, Bahrain, Kuwait, Qatar, Oman, and the United Arab Emirates. It is also common in Afghanistan and Iran. It has nothing to do with Islamic teachings and is considered to be an old cultural tradition.

**qibla:** The direction toward Mecca that a Muslim must face when he or she prays. Most mosques contain a niche in a wall that indicates the qibla.

**ramye al-jamarat:** Symbolic throwing of small stones during the **hajj** (q.v.) to signify the Muslims' defiance of the devil.

**Rashidun:** The "rightly guided" **caliphs** (q.v.), comprised of the four closest companions of the Prophet Muhammad: Abou Bakr, Omar, Othman, and Ali.

**riba:** Taking of interest, or usury, that is generally forbidden in Islamic jurisprudence (**fiqh**, q.v.).

**sakina:** Tranquility, serenity, and a feeling of the Divine Presence. Related to the Hebrew word *shekinah* that's part of the Jewish Kabbalah tradition.

**salaam:** Peace and submission.

**sewaak:** Wooden twig of certain trees that were used on a regular basis by Muslims for centuries to maintain oral hygiene.

**sharia:** Islamic law. Also the "way" or "path" that refers to the way Muslims should live or the righteous path they should follow. Sharia is derived from the Quran and traditions (**hadith**, q.v.) gathered from the life of the Prophet

Muhammad. Every single source of Islamic law is the result of human, not divine, effort.

**Shia:** The second largest denomination of Islam after **Sunni** (s.v.) Islam. The followers of Shia Islam are called Shias, but are also known as Shiites. Shia is the short form of the historic phrase *Shi-at Ali*, meaning "the followers of Ali" or "the faction of Ali," the cousin and son-in-law of the Prophet. Similar to other sects in Islam, Shia is based on the teachings of the Quran and the message of Muhammad, but with slight variations and interpretations. At present, there are more than seventy sects in Islam.

**shura:** Consultation.

**Sufi:** A practitioner of the Sufism tradition in Islam. Sufism is the inner, mystical dimension of the Muslim faith. The word Sufi is believed to have originated from *suf*, which means "wool" or "coarse wool garments," which the first Sufis in Medina wore as an emblem of their poverty and detachment from the world. Some scholars have also suggested that Sufi is a corruption of the Greek word *sophia*, or "wisdom."

**sunna:** Habit or usual practice. The Muslim usage of this term refers to the sayings and living habits of the Prophet Muhammad, which were recorded some 150 years after his death.

**Sunni:** The largest sect of Islam, comprising at least 85 percent of the world's 1.57 billion Muslims. Sunnis are also referred to as Ahl al-sunna, "people of the tradition of Muhammad." The word Sunni comes directly from **sunna** (q.v.). The major schools of Sunni thought (*madhahib*) are: Hanafi, Shafii, Malaki, and Hanbali, with Hanbali being the strictest.

**sura:** Chapter in the Quran.

**tajdid:** Renewal. In an Islamic context, tajdid refers to the revival of Islam in order to purify and reform society, to move it toward greater equity and justice.

**tashkil:** Name for the signs indicating the vowels in Arabic scripts, such as the Quran. They were apparently unknown in pre-lslamic times. These signs help to determine the correct pronunciation of Arabic words. These signs were introduced into the Quranic script during the time of the Umayyad caliph, Abdel-Malik ibn Marawan and during the governorship of al-Hajjaj ibn Yusuf in Iraq around the year 705.

**umma:** Community or nation. It is commonly used to mean either the collective nation of states—or in the context of Pan-Arabism, the whole Arab world. In the context of Islam, the word umma represents the "community of the believers" (*ummat al-muemineen*), or the whole Muslim world.

**Wahhabis:** Founded by the **Sunni** (q.v.) fundamentalist Sheikh Muhammad ibn abdel-Wahhab in the 1700s in what is present-day Saudi Arabia. There is a sharp distinction between the Wahhabi form of Islam and the original teachings of the Prophet Muhammad. The Wahhabis are considered by the vast majority of Muslims to be the main cause for militant extremism in the world today, and are not considered by any means to be representatives of Islam. Other extremist groups that claim to be connected to Islam include al-Qaeda, Salafis, and the Taliban, among others. The Taliban are notoriously known for their horrific human rights violations against women. The first

Muslim extremists were the Kharijites, who originated in Basra (present-day Iraq) at around 655.

**wajib:** Obligatory or religious duty. It is one of the five types or categories of approval (ahkam) into which Islamic jurisprudence categorizes the acts of Muslims. It is used interchangeably with the word **fard** (q.v.).

**wudu:** Ablution; the Islamic act of washing parts of the body with water. Muslims are required to be clean in preparation for ritual prayers.

**zaka:** Almsgiving. One of the Five Pillars of Islam, it is the mandatory giving of 2.5 percent of one's net income as charity to the poor and needy. It is often compared to the system of tithing and alms, but it serves principally as a welfare contribution to poor and deprived Muslims.

# Recommended Reading

In addition to the sources that are quoted and mentioned in this book, I would like to suggest to the reader the following books related to Islam:

## INTRODUCTION TO ISLAM

Abou el-Fadl, Khaled. *The Search for Beauty in Islam: A Conference of the Books.* Lanham, MD: Rowman & Littlefield, 2005.

Ali-Karamali, Sumbul. *The Muslim Next Door: The Quran, the Media, and that Veil Thing.* Ashland, OR: White Cloud Press, 2008.

Aslan, Reza. *No god But God: The Origins, Evolution, and Future of Islam.* New York: Random House, 2005.

Chebel, Malek. *Symbols of Islam.* New York: Barnes & Noble Books, 1999.

Esposito, John. *Voices of Resurgent Islam.* Oxford: Oxford University Press, 1983.

Wheeler, Brannon. *Teaching Islam*. New York: Oxford University Press, 2003.

## The Quran

Abou Khalil, Shauqi. *Atlas of the Quran: Places, Nations, Landmarks*. Riyadh, Saudi Arabia: Darussalam, 2003.

Asad, Muhammad (trans. and ed.). *The Message of the Quran*. Gibraltar: Dar al-Andalus, 1980.

Bucaille, Maurice. *The Bible, the Quran and Science: The Holy Scriptures Examined in the Light of Modern Knowledge*. Elmhurst, NY: Tahrike Tarsile Quran, 2003.

Salles, Michael. *Approaching the Quran: The Early Revelations*. Ashland, OR: White Cloud Press, 1999.

## Western Views of Islam

Blanks, David, and Michael Frassetto. *Western Views of Islam in Medieval and Early Modern Europe*. New York: St. Martin's Press, 1999.

Daniel, Norman. *Islam and the West: The Making of an Image*. Edinburgh: Edinburgh University Press, 1960.

Hourani, Albert. *Islam in European Thought*. Cambridge: Cambridge University Press, 1991.

Kabbani, Rana. *Europe's Myths of the Orient*. London: Pandora Press, 1994.

Masud, Enver. *The War on Islam*. Arlington, VA: The Wisdom Fund, 2008.

Said, Edward. *Orientalism: Western Conceptions of the Orient*. New York: Random House, 1979.

Zakzouk, Mahmoud. *Islam in the Mirror of Western Thought.* Cairo: Dar al-Fikr al-Araby, 1994.

### EXTREMISM AND FUNDAMENTALISM

Appelby, Scott, ed. *Spokesmen for the Despised: Fundamentalist Leaders of the Middle East.* Chicago: The University of Chicago Press, 1997.

Armstrong, Karen. *The Battle for God.* New York: Ballantine, 2000.

Choueiri, Youssef. *Islamic Fundamentalism.* London: Continuum, 1990.

Esposito, John. *Unholy War: Terror in the Name of Islam.* Oxford: Oxford University Press, 2002.

Lawrence, Bruce. *Defenders of God: The Fundamentalist Revolt Against the Modern Age.* New York: I. B. Tauris, 1990.

### WOMEN AND ISLAM

Anway, Carol. *Daughters of Another Path: Experiences of American Women Choosing Islam.* Lee's Summit, MO: Yawna Publications, 1995.

Barlas, Asma. *Believing Women in Islam: Unreading Patriarchal Interpretations of the Quran.* Austin, TX: University of Texas Press, 2002.

Ebrahimji, Maria, and Zahra Suratwala, ed. *I Speak for Myself: American Women on Being Muslim.* Ashland, OR: White Cloud Press, 2011.

Esposito, John, and Natana DeLong-Bas. *Women in Muslim Family Law.* Syracuse, NY: Syracuse University Press, 1982.

Wadud, Amina. *Inside the Gender Jihad: Women's Reform in Islam.* New York: Oxford University Press, 2006.

————. *Quran and Woman: Rereading the Sacred Text from a Woman's Perspective.* New York: Oxford University Press, 1999.

## Muslims in America

Findley, Paul. *Silent No More: Confronting America's False Images of Islam.* Beltsville, MD: Amana Publications, 2001.

Lang, Jeffery. *Struggling to Surrender: Some Impressions of an American Convert to Islam.* Beltsville, MD: Amana Publications, 1994.

## The Middle East

Braverman, Mark. *Fatal Embrace: Christians, Jews and the Search for Peace in the Holy Land.* Austin, TX: Synergy Books, 2010.

el-Ghonemy, M. Riad. *Affluence and Poverty in the Middle East.* Oxford: Routledge, 1998.

Lewis, Bernard. *The Crisis of Islam: Holy War and Unholy Terror.* New York: Random House, 2004.

————. *The Middle East.* New York: Touchstone, 1997.

————. *What Went Wrong?: The Clash Between Islam and Modernity in the Middle East.* New York: Oxford University Press, 2002.

## Islamic Finance

Ayub, Muhammad. *Understanding Islamic Finance.* Chichester, England: John Wiley & Sons, 2008.

Warde, Ibrahim. *Islamic Finance in the Global Economy.* Edinburgh: Edinburgh University Press, 2000.

## SUFISM AND SPIRITUALITY

Barks, Coleman, and Michael Green. *The Illuminated Prayer: The Five-Times Prayer of the Sufis.* New York: Ballantine, 2000.

Chittick, William. *The Sufi Path of Love: The Spiritual Teachings of Rumi.* Albany, NY: State University of New York Press, 1983.

Yusuf, Hamza. *Purification of the Heart: Signs, Symptoms and Cures of the Spiritual Diseases of the Heart.* Burr Ridge, IL: Starlatch Press, 2004.

## THE SIMILARITIES BETWEEN JUDAISM, CHRISTIANITY, AND ISLAM

Dirks, Jerald. *The Abrahamic Faiths: Judaism, Christianity, and Islam: Similarities and Contrasts.* Beltsville, MD: Amana Publications, 2006.

Ghounem, Muhammad. *200+ Ways the Quran Helps the Bible: How Islam Unites Judaism and Christianity.* Newtown, CT: MMNC, 2003.

Menocal, Maria Rosa. *The Ornament of the World: How Muslims, Jews, and Christians Created a Culture of Tolerance in Medieval Spain.* Boston: Back Bay Books, 2002.

## THE CRUSADES

Armstrong, Karen. *Holy War: The Crusades and Their Impact on Today's World.* New York: Doubleday, 1991.

Hillenbrand, Carole. *The Crusades: Islamic Perspectives.* Oxford: Routledge, 2000.

Maalouf, Amin. *The Crusades Through Arab Eyes.* London: Al-Saqi Books, 1984.

## WEB SITES

I'm a big proponent of constructive criticism and productive interfaith dialogue, but unfortunately, there is a great deal of false information and destructive rhetoric against Islam in the Western media, especially on the Internet. Therefore, the reader may wish to view the following web sites that reflect the authentic spirit of Islam and promote interfaith objectivity:

About.com: Islam. The New York Times Company. http://islam.about.com/.

Charter for Compassion. http://charterforcompassion.org/.

Council on American-Islamic Relations. http://www.cair.com/.

Georgetown University. The Prince Alwaleed Bin-Talal Center for Muslim-Christian Understanding. "Building bridges of understanding for more than a decade." http://cmcu.georgetown.edu/.

Hussein abd el-Waheed Amin. "Promoting the theology of Islam." IslamForToday.com. http://www.islamfortoday.com/.

Muslim Public Affairs Council. "Making Muslims part of the solution since 1988." http://www.mpac.org/.

The Institute of Interfaith Dialogue. http://www.interfaith-dialog.org/.

The True Call. "A paradigm shift: A guide for those seeking the truth." http://www.thetruecall.com/.

The University of Georgia's Virtual Center for Interdisciplinary Studies of the Islamic World (VCISIW). http://www.uga.edu/islam/.

Zaytuna College. http://www.zaytuna.org/.

**Note:** For various reasons, the content of these web sites may change, or the web sites may not be available on the Internet on the date of publication of this book.

# Index

12234998R00196

Made in the USA
Lexington, KY
30 November 2011